The Cock Still Crows

Also by Induk Pahk

The Cock Still Crows

Induk Pahk

VANTAGE PRESS
New York   Washington   Atlanta   Hollywood

Excerpts from the *Revised Standard Version of the Bible*, © 1946, 1952, 1971, 1973, used by permission.

Published by Vantage Press, Inc.
516 West 34th Street, New York, New York 10001

Manufactured in the United States of America
Standard Book Number 533-02656-3

To my friends in North America
with gratitude and love

PREFACE

For two hundred years, the United States of America has been a nation. I have shared one-fourth of her life. I first came to America fifty years ago—a schoolgirl still, although I was already a wife and mother. America took me to her heart!

I write this book to express deep gratitude to my friends in the United States and Canada for what they have meant to me and what they have done for me and for my people in Korea for half a century.

My first book, *September Monkey,* portrayed the indomitable faith and undefeatible determination of a remarkable woman—my mother—who gave me an education despite the weighty traditions and accumulated conventions of male-dominated Korea. I was her life and career.

Reflecting her vision, I was able to realize my own dream of educating young Koreans by establishing Berea in Korea—Induk Vocational High School—with thirty boys in the tenth grade in 1964. As I followed in my mother's footsteps, there were countless obstacles and difficulties; with God's help, I managed to surmount them all. That story is told in my second book, *The Hour of the Tiger.*

This book, *The Cock Still Crows,* reveals how each step was taken miraculously until my dream of Berea in Korea became a living reality—growing year by year to accommodate 2000 boys in the Vocational High School in 1976. It has branched out into a coeducational junior college—Induk Institute of Design—which combines art and technology with the aim of restoring the luster to Korean craftsmanship.

The eighty-fourth Congress of the United States gave me a key to America—a permanent visa—in 1955, and my friends prepared many stages for me to play my role. The playwright and director of this production is the Almighty God.

I want to express special appreciation to Lily Houseman, my friend and secretary of the Berea in Korea Foundation, who went over my rough draft untiringly with understanding and discernment. Earl E. Houseman, Lily's husband, examined the entire first draft from a man's point of view, whereas their son Earl A. considered it from a young man's angle. Their neighbor, Dr. Fern Stukenbroeker, read the draft, also. The final manuscript was carefully prepared by Margaret Blackledge. All contributed valuable comments and suggestions, and I sincerely thank them. I feel this book should be called a book of all generations.

The Cock Still Crows

CHAPTER I

God gave me a dream that will not let me sleep;
He gave me an adventure that will not let me rest.
That dream, that adventure,
Unfolds step by step.

—Induk Pahk

"We are going to die! We are going to die! We are going to die!"

Those words—in Chinese, in Japanese, in Korean—assailed me on all sides. The ship pitched and tossed. The sixteen women sharing the steerage compartment with me clung to their bunks, retching and moaning. The sour smells enveloped me.

I thought of Jonah, running from God, caught in a storm at sea as we were caught. Was I Jonah? Was this storm because of me? The moans around me rose and fell with the motion of the ship, but I knew that I was not running away. I was going where God willed. Without His direct intervention in my life, I would not be here.

We were not going to die!

It has been fifty years since I lived through that storm on an unstabilized liner in the middle of the Pacific Ocean. I was on my way to America for the first time, armed with a scholarship to Wesleyan College in Macon, Georgia, to continue an education begun in childhood in the mission schools in Korea.

1

I have made the trip between Korea and America more than twenty times since, always with God at my side. With my precious permanent visa, I spend most of my time in America, speaking constantly on behalf of "Berea in Korea," my dream-come-true for educating Korean youth.

As the cock heralds the dawn, so my dream was born in the morning of my life; now, in the evening, the cock still crows!

According to our ancient Oriental zodiac, 1976 is the Year of the Dragon. This mythological beast is known in Korea as the king of the ocean as the tiger is king of the mountain. Anyone born under the sign of the dragon, be it year, month, day, or hour, is born to be great.

The dragon has only one goal: to find the "pearl of great price." Where is it? It is somewhere at the bottom of the sea—but in what part? The dragon plunges into the ocean, exploring, searching, looking around carefully and tenaciously until it finds the pearl. Although it takes an entire lifetime, the dragon never gives up. When the great day comes, it clutches the pearl of great price in its claws, returns to the surface of the ocean, and soars into the sky, announcing proudly, "I have found it!"

How it thrilled me when my mother told me the dragon story! "You were born on the day of the dragon," she continued. "Whatever you dream, I am afraid it will take your lifetime, but don't ever give up until you achieve like a dragon."

A dream is like the oak which sleeps in the acorn or the bird that waits in the egg. It is like a tiny spark which can set a great forest on fire, or a small rudder which can make a big ship turn in any direction the pilot wishes in spite of a strong wind. How powerful a dream is! Every great achievement was first and for a time a dream. One of the most thrilling moments for a design engineer comes when he tests his creative work. A dream is the seedling of reality. "Where there is no vision, the people perish."

One's original dream may change, owing to circumstances, interests, or necessity. I have quite a number of friends who say that what they are doing is not their main dream. They are trapped—caught in a net of circumstance. But I say, no experience is without value—it may be the needed tempering to steel one's resolve.

My daughter Iris Kim is a perfect example. Her dream was to become a musician—a pianist. She entered Ewha College, the first girls' school in Korea, founded by a Methodist missionary, Mrs. Mary Scranton, in 1886. There were no girls' schools in Korea's long history of four thousand years until Ewha came into being. Up to this time, every home served as a school for girls, where they learned cooking, sewing, etiquette, how to rear a family, and how to get along with all the in-laws. Patience and obedience were the prime requisites. It was the curriculum prescribed by tradition and Confucianism.

Iris and I learned a new curriculum, planned and worked out on behalf of women. In the new light of the Christian faith, Iris was able to find her talent, using the piano as her instrument. She developed her gift to the fullest, so that she was known as the Haydn of Korea.

After the Korean War, she came to America with her two little boys to continue with her music. She registered at Catholic University of America in Washington, D.C., to study the pipe organ. She had never touched the pipe organ in Korea because she was unable to find one on which to practice; but during United Nations Week in October, 1962, she gave a pipe organ recital at the Washington National Cathedral.

My own dream came true when I founded Induk Vocational High School (Berea in Korea) in Seoul in 1964 with thirty boys in the tenth grade. One day, Iris asked me if she could visit the school I had founded. At this time, she played the pipe organ on Sundays at the Korean Church which met in the Foundry United Methodist Church in Washington. In addition, she taught quite a number of Korean children the piano at home. She was fully engaged in music and loved it. She made her piano sing, sigh, and speak. Michelangelo said, "It is only well with me when I have a chisel in my hand." Iris was almost like him when she had a piano in front of her.

One day she said, "Mother, I want to go to Korea and see how our school is doing." It was administered at that time by her cousin, Nam-Kyu Chung.

I replied, "You may go and see it while I take care of your two little sons. But don't ever think you have to take over the administration."

She didn't commit herself one way or the other, but took off on May 12, 1965, from Friendship Airport. She was gone six months. I knew then that she was sizing up the whole project—whether she could take over the school physically, spiritually, technically, and even emotionally. If she did, she would have to leave her two fatherless boys with the "outside grandmother" who traveled all the time speaking on behalf of her school.

In Korea there is a distinction between one's father's mother and one's mother's mother. All of the father's side is "inside," whereas the mother's side is "outside." Iris's boys were my "outside grandsons." Aside from the emotional problem of leaving the boys, the real issue was whether she had administrative ability. She finally decided to leave her first love—music—and take over the school. Depending solely on God's wisdom, given freely and without reproach, she made her decision quietly and prayerfully.

While Iris was making her serious decision in Korea, I had my difficulties with her boys—or, rather, with their stomachs. Discipline was not a big problem because they were still small enough to mind me, but cooking was entirely foreign to me; and when I was at home, I had to prepare their meals. The only things I knew how to make were toast and boiling water—the toaster and the kettle did all the work! I never cease to thank God for the inventors of these gadgets! What a pleasure it is to hear the singing of a boiling kettle. A friend of mine once said, "Be like a tea kettle. When up to your neck in hot water, keep on singing!"

Even simple cooking was a problem for me. One Saturday morning, I decided to give my outside grandsons a treat—pancakes, bacon, and eggs. I bought Aunt Jemima pancake mix and a bottle of syrup. I read the directions carefully—or so I thought! But I dumped the whole box at once into a bowl and mixed in the milk, eggs, and shortening. Of course, I knew immediately that I had far too much. Quietly I scooped out enough for the three of us and put the rest into the refrigerator. We had pancakes for several more meals!

From this experience I learned a great lesson. Everyone—man or woman, boy or girl—should learn simple cooking. Now my two grandsons know how to cook like American boys. I often say that if I were a young man looking for a wife, I would ask the prospective girl whether she liked to cook. If she said no, that would be the end of the romance. But it doesn't work out that way. Love does not proceed with calm reason. Am I not right?

While I was going through some turbulent days in cooking, purely through my stupidity, Iris returned to America with a firm decision to run the school. Of course, I was glad to give her my cooking job, even for six weeks. She was to return to her post early in January, soon after the annual board meeting of the Berea in Korea Foundation.

I asked Iris, "How are you going to run the school? Your dream and your goal have always been music."

5

She responded to my question with four words, "With my little baton. You see, mother, I learned to conduct a choir with a little baton. The school is my choir. All I need to know is which teacher needs my baton stronger or softer. According to his temperament, I use either pianissimo or fortissimo. In turn, each teacher uses his baton with his class. But I use my little baton with love and understanding, and I ask them to do the same."

Iris was one hundred percent right. Success is falling in love with one's work, and bringing out the best in each person one touches. I felt she meant what she said. Some say what they don't mean; some say what they mean; and some mean what they say. Iris comes in this last category—she means what she says. She has developed into a strong and powerful principal of our Induk Vocational High School, well able to take on the added responsibility as president of our new junior college, Induk Institute of Design.

Some people have a dream but give it up because they cannot meet the challenge. Others may not recognize their dream when they are young, but live vaguely dissatisfied lives, continually looking for "something" to fulfill their desire and aim in life.

I have a friend who did find that "something." He is C. Pendleton Lewis, rector of Calvary Church, in Stonington, Connecticut. Following graduation from Harvard, he took a position with a New York bank, married, and became the father of a son and two daughters. He was a naval officer in World War II, receiving a Bronze Star for his part in the invasion of Okinawa.

Still searching when he returned from the war, he and his family moved to a dairy farm near Falls Village, Connecticut, and became involved in Trinity Church. There he found that "something" for which he had been looking—his pearl of great price. At the age of thirty-nine, he entered divinity school and was subsequently ordained to the priesthood.

Mr. Lewis offered a powerful prayer for our foundation when I visited his church. He had heard of my struggling efforts to finance Berea in Korea without specific denominational backing. Our friends' prayers play a very real part in the success of our schools.

My experience with my dream was different from that of either Iris or my minister friend C. Pendleton Lewis. I had one and only one dream in my youth—going to America.

Dreams change and expand as we progress through life. As one is fulfilled, another wider one takes its place. My dream now is helping the young people of Korea through our schools. But its foundation is my earlier dream—going to America. I dreamed of it for ten years. When the time arrived for me to go—armed with a passport, passage money, and a full scholarship from Ohio Wesleyan, I let my golden opportunity pass by. There must have been a powerful force to dislodge me from my ten years of burning desire. Indeed there was! Love, even an unwise love, is the most powerful force in the world!

I was only six years old when I first heard of America, on my first Christmas Day in a country church in Korea. My Confucian father and my only brother, three years younger than I, had both died of cholera earlier that year. According to Korean custom, women had no right of inheritance, and a nephew was selected to be my mother's "son" and inherit my father's estate. Mother was unwilling to accept this solution, and turned to a Christian cousin for advice.

He knew my mother was a Buddhist, an expert weaver, and a farmer. He also knew what mother needed at this dark and desperate hour in her life. She needed consolation and hope.

Mother's cousin helped her get those two things

needed in life by urging her to go to his church. He told her, "God loves you, and He knows you need a son. If you accept God's way, you can educate your daughter, and she can take your son's place."

Following our cousin's direction, one bitterly cold morning mother and I walked three miles to the mission church. It was Christmas Day. The first three Protestant missionaries from America had arrived in Korea on another Christian holy day, Easter Sunday in 1885. Of course, I heard the name of Jesus in Korean—*Yeasoo*.

But the most unforgettable thing was a No. 2 yellow pencil and a yellow writing pad put into my hand as a Christmas present. It was intended for a boy, but the gifts of handkerchiefs for the girls ran out when it came to my turn. So the lady handed over to me one leftover boy's present, the pencil and pad.

The pencil and pad came from America, we were told. It was the first time I had heard of *Meegook* (America). That strange name, *Meegook*, embedded itself in my little mind and became a spark as I grew up. I still remember my question to my mother, "How far is *Meegook*?"

She replied, "I do not know; it is far, far away, but the missionaries came all the way to Korea from *Meegook*."

The pencil and pad proved to be not only seedlings for my imagination but also the simple tools to test my brain. Here I must tell how we celebrate a boy's first birthday in Korea. The main purpose of the celebration is to see which article the baby picks up first, as this determines his future. His grandmother dresses him beautifully in colorful clothing and sets him on a cushion. On a table in front of him are several objects—books, pencils, notebooks, rice, money, thread—along with delectable cakes and fruits.

The tense moment arrives. Grandparents, parents, uncles, aunts, and all the other relatives and friends wonder what he will reach for first. If he picks up a book, with one accord they all say, "Oh, he is going to be a scholar." They all rejoice about his future. If he chooses rice, people say he is to be a farmer, and so on. The amusing part of it all is that his grandfather pushes a desired object close to his grandson for him to pick. But the baby is unpredictable—he reaches for an article farther away.

This kind of celebration was for boys only—not for girls, because a girl's destiny was mapped out from birth. However, a girl's first birthday was celebrated with beautiful clothing and a feast, as well. As for me, God put into my hand a pencil and a pad on his son's birthday, Christmas; I didn't even have to pick them up. It was prophetic that I should write a book with that pencil and pad years later.

The kindling of my dream of going to America caught fire when I went to Ewha High School in Seoul at the age of twelve. Living in a mission school where the American missionary teachers lived and taught made America more real to me. There I started learning the ABC's, using the first reader that came from America. From that time on, I was in an American environment saturated with Christian ideals and teachings. Furthermore, I had correspondence with two friends—one blind friend, C. G. Steinhart, who provided my tuition to Ewha, and Thelma Coullie, of Pittsburgh, Pennsylvania. I still have a photostatic copy of a letter I wrote to her in 1918. Soon after my first book *September Monkey* was published, she located me and sent me a copy. Later I met her at a friend's home. What a memorable day it was!

I was graduated from Ewha College and taught until the Korean Independence Movement broke out on March 1, 1919. It was soon after the Paris Peace Conference where Woodrow Wilson presented his famous fourteen points. One of them was "self-determination of

9

peoples." Korea was under Japanese occupation then. We have a saying, "No baby gets milk unless he cries." So we cried for our independence.

It was the first peaceful people's movement in Korean history, well-organized and staged on the funeral day of our last, ill-fated king. Every Korean—young and old, man and woman—joined in this independence movement. Japanese police started arresting Koreans. I, too, was arrested and taken to Westgate Prison in Seoul.

Since I was considered responsible for "inciting" my students, I was put into solitary confinement in a small cell about six-by-six foot with a nine-foot ceiling. I felt as if I were buried alive in a tomb. A cold March wind howled through the trap door.

Three times a day, I was given a glob of cooked soybeans liberally mixed with grains of sand and a dish of soup that looked as if it came from the sewer. Remembering mother's words, "Pray for your needs, not your wants," I started praying for two definite needs: food for my physical body and the Holy Bible for my spirit.

I prayed in this manner for weeks with no answer. At last I prayed with all my might, saying, "God, will you please send me the food and the English Bible? Someday you may need me." The next day, both came. I was astounded!

The food was from my dear college president Lulu E. Frey, the Bible from Dr. B. W. Billings, a Methodist missionary living next-door to Ewha. They knew what I needed most at that particular time and place.

After five months I was released on bond, then arrested again and imprisoned for one month more. Although my prospects of going to America were getting dim, my dream was getting more vivid. From a Korean point of view, it was hope against hope. The Japanese officials didn't like the American missionaries because they loved the Korean people. I know deep in my heart that no one can stop the changing seasons. When spring returns, winter has to give up. When one's plan coincides with God's, no one can stop it. With this firm belief, I was released from prison.

Upon my return to Ewha from the Japanese prison, who came to see me first? It was one of my students, Young Sook Kim, my favorite. She brought me a letter and a box of ginseng roots from her brother. She was a beautiful girl with a fair complexion, black wavy hair and dimples. I was delighted to see her and thrilled to get a letter and a gift box from her brother. I had never before had a letter from a young man.

I opened the letter; it was an invitation to his birthday party. He thanked me for my imprisonment in solitary confinement for the sake of Korea's Independence Movement.

I was safe in accepting his invitation because Young Sook told me Julia Syn was also invited. Julia and I both taught at Ewha and were both imprisoned, although she shared her cell with other Ewha girls. Julia was in the fourth class of Ewha College and graduated alone as I had in the third class, so we were very close. Julia later went to Ohio Wesleyan University, earned her A.B. degree, and met and married a fine young Korean man who became bishop of the Korean Methodist church.

On the designated day Julia and I went to Young Sook's home, on foot because it was nearby. When we arrived, Young Sook and her brother Woon Ho greeted us cordially. Then his mother and two other sisters welcomed us. They lived in a tile-roofed house in a desirable neighborhood. Woon Ho looked much like his sister. He was an athletic type, well-built, with black wavy hair, and was quite tall for a Korean. He had all the qualities a young girl would fall for at first sight.

I learned, at the dinner table, that Woon Ho played football at Pae Chae Boys' High School, a brother school of Ewha High School for girls. Both schools had been

11

founded by American Methodist missionaries. Furthermore, he loved music. Although he had had no lessons, he read music and sang any part beautifully. I also love music and used to sing contralto and play the accompaniment, so Woon Ho and I had at least one thing in common—love of music. It is easy to see why our daughter Iris is so talented in music.

At the table, Woon Ho and I sat across from each other. Julia and his mother faced each other. The two older girls waited on the table and the youngest sister was a little girl, shy and quiet, who just looked at the guests. There were dishes of charcoal-broiled beef, vegetables, bean cakes, seaweed, and a few different *kimchis* (pickles). The conversation centered around Korea's independence. Woon Ho wanted to do all he could to liberate Korea from Japanese occupation, as Julia and I did. He talked about the political situation freely because he knew we were deeply involved. The proof was our imprisonment in Westgate Prison.

His mother listened quietly. She was dressed in white, the symbol of mourning for Woon Ho's father who had died within the year. She must have been in her late forties and looked very wise and understanding. I was to learn later that she did, indeed, possess those qualities.

We remained for two hours. Then Julia and I had to return to Ewha to prepare Sunday School lessons for the following day. Both of us taught at the Chung Dong Korean Methodist Church which was next door to Ewha. It was the first Methodist church built in Seoul by American missionaries, and was flanked on one side by Ewha and on the other by Pae Chae, Woon Ho's school.

As Julia and I arose from the dinner table, Woon Ho offered to accompany us to Ewha. Was I happy! I didn't want to leave him. The three of us put on our Western shoes, which are not like typical Korean shoes. No matter what type shoe one wears, we remove them when we enter a room. Korea has four different kinds: leather, straw, rubber, and wood. The straw and leather shoes have no heels, the rubber shoes have a very low heel, and the wooden clogs have high heels like stilts for walking in the rain.

With Woon Ho escorting us, Julia and I walked toward Ewha. It was late in September and the temperature was neither hot nor cold, just right. A three-quarter moon hung high in the sky and a soft breeze was blowing. As we walked in silence, I thought of my cherished dream of going to America. I said to myself, "I must not let anything interfere with my dream," but I must confess something was interfering. Otherwise, why did that mile seem so short?

When we arrived at the main gate, we stopped. It was a marvelous, rich moment when my eyes met Woon Ho's for just a few seconds under the soft, September moon. Just that one glimpse put my dream of going to America to the test.

Not long after the dinner party, Young Sook brought me a letter from her brother. If you have been in love, you will know how I felt. It is a most wonderful experience! It is so strong that one will do anything to possess his beloved. King Edward VIII gave up his throne for the woman he loved. I gave up my one and only dream of going to America for the man I loved.

The romance progressed through the winter, becoming stronger as the months passed. Early in May, mother invited Woon Ho to visit Duk Dong where she lived. I had mentioned him occasionally to mother who well knew my ultimate goal of going to America. But there was no prospect of that in sight, and I was of marriageable age. Mother decided to see if this young man was worthy of her only son-daughter for whom she had sacrificed her life.

After Woon Ho's visit, Mother told me, "Woon Ho is exceptionally handsome and very courteous, but he is not a practical young man. He appears to be a 'playboy'—a grownup teenager. In addition to that, you have a different cultural background. You have been a Christian ever since you were six, and all through your life you have had one dream and one goal—to serve God and your country. Woon Ho is a typical, self-centered Korean man. With him, having a good time comes first. You and he look in entirely different directions; you don't speak the same language. Can you cope with it all? Think over the whole matter carefully and prayerfully.

"You are deeply in love, and you will not hear what I say now," she continued, "but you will understand when you face actual married life. You cannot live on love always. Love has to be replaced by trust, confidence, give and take, mutual understanding, and sharing. This comes only from serving God and man."

What magnificent, wise advice! In spite of her advice, I made up my mind to marry, proving the old saying that love is blind. But I had an uneasy feeling that I was on a wrong road. Somehow, I did not feel happy about my decision. I should have been happy, but I was not.

Upon my return from home, Miss Alice Appenzeller, then president of Ewha, called me into her office. Since I was dean, I thought she wanted to discuss school matters. She knew I was going with Woon Ho, but she didn't know how serious I was.

She said, "We have chosen you to go to Ohio Wesleyan next fall to further your education. Sooner or later the reins of Ewha must be in the hands of Korean nationals. We American missionaries are here to train you girls in leadership. A full scholarship has been obtained from Ohio Wesleyan and you are our number one choice. Passage money from Korea to America, and return, has been given by an American couple who are interested in Ewha. I want you to apply for a passport as soon as possible. The deadline is the first part of August, because the college opens in the middle of September. I want you to get there a few weeks ahead of time so you can feel the new environment."

Was I stunned! However, I kept my feelings inside and told her I would do as she said. I could have told her no because I was to be married, but I didn't because of my uneasy feelings. I told Woon Ho about the door that had opened to America without my solicitation. Of course, he congratulated me because he knew of my ultimate goal in life—to go to America. But he had an answer.

"Everything has its own time—sowing seeds in the spring, reaping in the fall, enjoying crops in the winter," he said. "For you, now is the time for getting married. Why don't we get married and go to America together?"

"I have a good idea," I replied. "I will apply for a passport. If it is granted, I will know that it is God's will for me to go to American alone."

I doubted that I could get a passport, because I had been imprisoned by the Japanese as a political prisoner. In those days, getting a passport from the Japanese government was as hard as pulling a star out of the sky. Under such impossible conditions, if I did get one it would be a miracle. Then I would know which way I should go.

With such reasoning I applied for a passport and it was granted! I was never so dumbfounded in all my life as when Miss Appenzeller handed me the passport.

She said, "I want you to get ready for the trip to America. I knew it would be most difficult for you to get a passport because you were a political prisoner under the Japanese government, but you got it. You know who helped you get it, of course. It was God. No one can stop his power."

It was late in May when I got the passport. Soon Ewha closed for summer vacation, about the middle of

June. No one will ever know the agony I went through those three weeks because of the two roads laid out for me. I could take only one—not both. God's chosen way was clearly indicated, but the strong love for Woon Ho pulled me down as the weeks passed, and I was weakened.

I said to Woon Ho, "Yes, we will get married. I will not go to America without you."

With this decision, I went to see Miss Appenzeller. I said hesitantly, "Miss Appenzeller, I have made up my mind to get married instead of going to America." Then I laid my passport on her desk.

Miss Appenzeller was as dumbfounded at my decision as I had been when I got my passport. She was not prepared to receive such a negative response from me.

All she said was, "Are you sure of what you are doing? Why don't you go to America and study? Such a chance comes to one in a million, and God gave it to you. When you return to Korea, if you and Woon Ho are still in love, you can get married."

I got up slowly and told her that I was leaving for home to prepare for my wedding. As long as I live, I will never forget her last look. She had great hopes for me, and I turned her down. What a tragic scene it was!

I packed my things to leave Ewha for good. This was the place where I grew up for ten long years as a student and teacher. Now I was uprooting myself from the Christian, American soil and replanting into the old, traditional Korean life which was almost foreign to me. My mother had uprooted her old traditional ways and transplanted herself in the free Christian life, and she coveted the same freedom for me. We had both been happy in this new Christian life.

Before I left for the train, I had a couple of hours to spend in the school I loved. My mind was torn between the old, free, familiar life in the school I knew, and the new married life yet unknown. Of course, I had observed non-Christian married life, but I had never experienced it. I lay down on the couch and dozed. Suddenly, I heard a voice saying, "Be a missionary." It was audible but I could not tell whether I was awake or dreaming.

I got up and said, "I can be a missionary by being married." It was my first experience of this kind. But it came true nine years later when I traveled in America and Canada under the auspices of the Student Volunteer Movement as its first Oriental traveling secretary for two years (1928–1930). My picture came out in the *Japan Christian Graphic Monthly* with a big caption, "Mrs. Induk Pahk, first Oriental missionary to North America."

One torrential rainy day in July, 1920, Woon Ho and I were married at his home in the presence of a dozen friends. Both mother and Miss Appenzeller, who tried to persuade me to go to America, were absent. I closed the door leading to America and opened that of marriage all by myself. It was purely my own choice. I was aware of my new role as a wife, daughter-in-law, and one of many in-laws. Woon Ho had three brothers and four sisters. Five of them were married and lived near my mother-in-law.

I knew I couldn't compete with my three sisters-in-law in sewing and cooking, but I could use the knowledge I gained from Ewha, such as English and music. However, there were no openings during the first year of my married life. I don't think I could have coped with the situation had it not been for my mother-in-law. I should call her mother-in-love. She saw the whole predicament from my angle, and even did the cooking for me when my turn came. Woon Ho had no earning power whatsoever. None! Both of us were nothing but parasites.

In the midst of this sad and confusing situation, the arrival of our daughter Iris, a year after our marriage, was like the bright morning star announcing the dawn of a new day. It was a new day for me with great hope. "Iris" is a direct translation of the Korean name I gave her. Later I learned that Iris means rainbow in Greek mythology. I dedicated Iris to God to fulfill his purpose and plans through her.

After the birth of Iris, new doors opened for me to teach English and music in several schools. There were so many requests that I couldn't meet all the demands. I taught in three different schools all day long, Monday through Saturday. Two and a half years after Iris's birth, Lotus was born. I felt rich in having two beautiful, healthy girls.

Suddenly I thought of what my mother had said, "Never give up your dream. If you dream with God, it comes true." It had been five years since I was married and I had a full load—more than I could take care of financially, having two girls and a husband depending on me.

Would you like to know where and how I got courage to revive my old dream? One cold December morning I was on my way to Pae Wha Southern Methodist Girls' School to teach. I saw more than half a dozen men, each with an A-frame conveyor on his back, waiting for someone to ask them to carry heavy loads. If one got a job, he had to walk a long distance, carrying a heavy load upon the A-frame, for very little money. Of course, they were poorly dressed. A long-forgotten Bible phrase rang through my mind as I passed them: "Is it nothing to you, all who pass by?"

Compassion welled up in me, and I said quietly in my prayer, "God, give me a second chance to go to America where I can learn how to help all these helpless men's sons and grandsons. I will not forsake you this time, I promise you." I was really deeply hurt by the scene I saw at that particular time.

I remembered hearing how Jane Addams started

18

Hull House in Chicago. The story goes that Jane Addams saw a crowd of poor East Londoners rush out to buy rotten cabbage from a wagon. The people swarmed around the wagon, eating rotten cabbage because they were so hungry. Jane Addams was shocked and thought of the poor in Chicago where she lived. The result was Hull House, America's first settlement house.

Soon after I saw my particular scene of the poor men with the A-frames, a strange opportunity opened to me through Rubie Lee, who taught music at Pae Wha with me. She wrote to her sister in Georgia of my great desire to go to school in America. When God steps in, no one can stop it. I was offered a full scholarship to Wesleyan College in Macon, Georgia. Miraculously, I got a passport in thirteen days; my passage money ($60) came from my earnings. Both my husband and my mother agreed that I should go. My Red Sea was wide open because I approached it holding the hand of God.

Before my departure, I went to see my mother in Duk Dong where I had gone to Kim Sung-No's private school for boys for two winters. Kim Sung-No was still alive when I made the return trip. He was pleased to hear that I was finally going to America.

As for mother, she gave me a prophetic message. She said, "You were like a tree growing up beautifully well-balanced. But suddenly the top of the tree was cut off, so much so that it now looks lopsided, dwarfish, unbalanced, and ugly—by marriage to a man who pulled you down instead of helping you. But you have hope because you are leaving him. It will take thirty years to cover the top by letting the side branches grow fully. Just remember it will take thirty long years!

"Your daughter Iris will help you," she continued. "Educate her well."

What an astounding prophecy it was! It took exactly twenty-eight years to produce my first book *September Monkey*. My daughter Iris is helping me run our two schools, Induk Vocational High School and Induk Institute of Design (a coeducational junior college) in Seoul, Korea, as principal of the first and president of the second. I cannot help but remember what the Bible said, ". . . no prophecy ever came by the impulse of man, but by men moved by the Holy Spirit spoken from God" (2 Peter 1:21, RSV).

As I look back over those six years of my married life, it was as though I were living in a cocoon. It was time for me to change into a butterfly. Without a cocoon, a silkworm can never become a butterfly. How important a cocoon is to everyone!

CHAPTER II

So I run straight toward the goal
in order to win the prize.
—Philippians 3:14 (*Good News for Modern Man*)

We all have dreams big and small, particularly when we are young. My mother gave me a piece of wise advice in choosing a dream. She said, "Pick out the most worthy dream for your life and press on until it becomes a reality. For you, one dream is enough. I, too, had one—to educate you—and I have accomplished it." She concluded her golden advice with a Korean proverb: "When you dig a well, dig in one place until you get water."

My dream came from another Korean proverb: "If you plan for a year, plant a crop; for ten years, plant a tree; for one hundred years, build a school."

Once I found a definite goal, I should start digging. But with what? I had to have tools. Where could I get them? A mighty thought came to me: "With hand and head, create something out of nothing." Today this is our school motto, but I first thought of it many, many years ago.

Miraculously, during my senior year at Wesleyan College, in Macon, Georgia, a chance was given me to attend the Quadrennial Convention of the Student Volunteer Movement of North America. Three weeks before it was to begin, the wife of the college president, Mrs. William F. Quillian, invited me to her home.

21

"Induk, I want you to go to the Student Volunteer Movement Quadrennial Convention in Detroit, Michigan," she told me. "It will be a great experience for you. There will be hundreds of students coming from the United States and Canada, as well as representatives from Europe, Asia, Africa, and South America."

I asked what it would cost. In those days, people usually traveled by train. She told me it would require about $75 for both travel and hotel expenses.

"Mrs. Quillian, I'll see how much I can raise," I said. I had learned long before that heaven helps those who help themselves.

I explored the situation prayerfully. Like my mother, I asked God to give me an idea. A thought flashed through my mind—why not write to the secretary for Korean Students in America? The next morning I posted my letter, and by return mail he sent me a check for $25.

Right away I called on Mrs. Quillian and broke the news. "Mrs. Quillian, I got $25 from the Korean Student Fund in New York. Twenty-five dollars down and $50 to go!"

Her answer surprised me. "I have $25 too, given by our Wesleyan College Y.W.C.A."

I was sure now of going to Detroit, with two-thirds of the needed money on hand.

On December 28, 1927, six delegates from Wesleyan under the leadership of Eleanor Neill, professor of religious education, took the Dixie Flyer for Detroit, a seventeen-hour trip. I didn't have the last $25, but I knew it would be provided, someway, somehow, because I was sure of God's leading.

When we arrived, winter snow covered the whole city—streets, rooftops, everywhere. It was very, very cold for my fellow travelers because they were born and reared in the South. None of them had seen snow except me, for I was born in Korea and grew up where there were four seasons. I can still picture the girls shivering in the cold.

"Aren't you freezing to death, Induk?"

I said, "I *am* cold, but I'm used to it."

The next day we all registered at the newly opened Masonic Temple, convention headquarters. There were college and seminary students, professors and sponsors, members of the Y.M.C.A. and Y.W.C.A., and quite a number of overseas students from the Orient, Europe, and Africa—a total of 3000. I saw Chinese and Japanese students, both men and women, and some Korean students too, but they were all men. I was the only Korean woman present.

On the last day of the year, the day before the convention was to close, I still didn't have the $25 needed for my return ticket. The hour of departure was coming close.

On New Year's Eve, we Wesleyan girls went out to throw snowballs with some neighboring students from Georgia. When I returned to my room, there was a telegram under the door. I wondered who would send me a wire.

Quickly I opened it. It was from the headquarters of the Student Volunteer Movement, and read, "We have chosen you and two other delegates to speak to the entire convention tomorrow morning, for fifteen minutes, on the topic, 'What Christianity Means to Me!' Please be at the back of the main platform by 10:00 A.M. For this service, we will give you $25."

Do you wonder why I trust God completely?

I clutched the telegram and said, "God, did you know I needed $25 to go back to Wesleyan?"

"Of course I knew," I could hear him saying so clearly through my inner ear. "Didn't you ask me for it?"

I went to bed with a special thanksgiving prayer. With such a promise, how could I have spent my second

23

New Year's Eve in America any better? When I awakened on New Year's Day, I felt so exhilarated that all I could say was, "God, help me to honor and glorify you to the fullest this morning at the convention."

At 10:00 I went backstage in the Masonic Temple. There were two men students—one from Africa, the other from the Middle East—waiting to speak also. Right on the dot, I was led to the platform.

The minute I appeared, the clapping hands of 3000 people overwhelmed me. I was only five feet tall and weighed 105 pounds. I felt awe when I saw the 3000 sets of curious eyes focused on me. Of course, I had some experience speaking to Sunday School children and Wednesday-night prayer meetings in churches ever since I came to America, but these were all small groups—usually thirty to fifty, or at the most one hundred people—not such a crowd as this. I was overwhelmed!

Just before starting my first sentence, I flashed my wire to God: "Please speak through me."

I still remember what I said. Since it was January 1, I said "A Happy New Year," in Korean, then translated it into English, "A Happy New Year!" The whole convention responded enthusiastically. Then I told them that of the many important discoveries in the latter part of the nineteenth century the most important one was the discovery of Korean womanhood by American Protestant missionaries who established Ewha High School, the first school for girls in Korea's 4000-year history. More cheers came from the floor.

My third sentence was that because of Ewha, I graduated from college and came to America to further my education. Then I told how my mother had disguised me as a boy at the age of six and a half and sent me to a boys' school. With this story the crowd became quite excited over my adventure. I closed with my six months' imprisonment in solitary confinement under the

24

Japanese occupation. I expressed my dream to help Korean young men and women get a good, practical education. It took only eleven and a half minutes, with applause from the floor five different times. A student from Africa followed me. He used my leftover three and a half minutes plus his own fifteen. He was tall and spoke perfect English.

Why was I chosen from among the Oriental students? The story goes that if a Chinese student were chosen, the Japanese wouldn't like it, and vice versa. Why not a woman from Korea? I do not know how accurate this is, but from a psychological point of view I would say it was a wise move. It sometimes pays off to be a woman from a country such as mine at such a time. ". . . strength out of weakness," the Bible says.

Two months later, I was called into President Quillian's office to meet a gentleman from New York. I thought to myself, "It must be a very important matter, otherwise he wouldn't have come to see me all the way from New York." And it was!

My visitor was Weyman C. Huckabee, from the Student Volunteer Movement (S.V.M.) headquarters in New York. He said, "We have had many requests from colleges in the United States and Canada for your appearance on their campuses. We would like to have you as a traveling secretary. If at all possible, I want you to accept the invitation. The pay will be $75 a month, nine months of the year. We will take care of your travel expenses while you are with us. We want you to join us in September."

I replied, "What an honor it is to be asked by the S.V.M. to be the first Oriental traveling secretary. But how about my visa? As you know, I have a student visa."

He said, "Don't worry about it. No problem. We will take care of it. All we want from you is your positive answer, yes."

I continued, "My plan after graduation was to study

for one more year on my graduate work."

"You can kill two birds with one stone. You can work on your master's degree during the summer months and travel during the school year. It will take you a bit longer, but if I were you I would accept the S.V.M. offer. It will be such a tremendous experience, valuable to your future plans. You said in your speech that you wanted to help Korean young people with their education, did you not?"

I replied, "Yes, I did."

All this time Dr. Quillian kept quiet and listened. I was sure he did not want to interfere with my decision one way or the other. When I said, "Mr. Huckabee, I will accept your offer," Dr. Quillian congratulated me on my wise decision. He said, "Such a chance comes only to a few, and it came to you through the grace of God whom you trust and obey."

Mr. Huckabee and I parted, to meet again at the next S.V.M. Council meeting which was to be held at Kalamazoo College in Michigan the first part of September. In the meantime, he was to get an extension on my visa for my new post.

That night I went out on the porch of the Wesleyan dorm and watched the stars while my mind recreated the scene in Dr. Quillian's office that afternoon. It was spring in Macon and the weather was neither cold nor hot, just right—perfect. The gentle breeze brought to my face the blended fragrance of azaleas, dogwood, tulips, magnolias, daffodils, hyacinths, and, of course, Georgia peach blossoms.

In the midst of this paradise, I looked up at the moon, and it was a three-quarter moon, just as it had been when I walked to Ewha with my first and only love, Woon Ho Kim, exactly seven years before. On that stage, a young man and a young girl met and a strong human love pulled them together . . . so much so that I was willing to give up my dearest dream in behalf of my love for the young man. But this night, on another college campus, I fell in love not with one young man but with the young men and women of Korea collectively. I did not see them in person as I had Woon Ho, but my desire for their education was so strong that I couldn't stop it. From that night on, my ultimate goal was to help Korean youth to get an education. I did not know then that it was a life-consuming proposition, but I realized many unpredicted problems would accompany my new love.

When I married, the wedding ceremony took only fifteen minutes, yet problem after problem followed. Sometimes, I felt I could never go through it for another day. But this new love would bring much, much bigger problems. At that moment, the greatest hope of tackling the new venture came from the Bible, "I can do all things through Christ who strengthens me." Practically, I lived with this thought not only in my waking moments but even in my sleep.

This idea of educating Korea's youth came to my mind when I took a course in education at Ewha. On my Ewha College commencement day, I was to prophesy concerning my goal in life. I said I wanted to be like the famous Swiss educator, Pestalozzi. His motto was "All for others—for myself, nothing." I wanted to be an educator as he was. My second wish was to be the Demosthenes of Korea—a great orator.

Demosthenes aroused my imagination when I read the story of how he disciplined and trained himself to become the greatest orator in Greece, despite great odds. His voice was weak and unpleasant, and one shoulder was hunched higher than the other. Yet he had the will to overcome all his defects. He practiced talking with pebbles in his mouth, and to strengthen his voice he competed with the roaring waves on the beach. To overcome his habit of hitching up one shoulder, he hung a sword that would touch the shoulder if he raised it. Finally, he became known as the greatest of all orators. I was attracted to his story because I feel anything worthwhile is worth great effort to attain.

Some people never reach their goal, but the effort itself is worthwhile. My father was one of those. His dream was to pass the royal examination given once or twice a year by the king. If one came out on top, he would be given high honor—perhaps even becoming prime minister of the king's government. He would have thrust upon him glory, honor, fame, and wealth. Every young man of that time dreamed the same dream— climbing the political ladder to the top.

My father studied Chinese classics from childhood on. Finally, he was ready to take the royal examination. He walked all the way to Seoul, about 180 miles from our village. The journey took weeks. Father failed and returned home to study some more. He made a second trip to Seoul and failed again. He repeated the trip a third time without reaching his goal. Mother told me he might have tried again and again until he succeeded, but the institution of the royal examination was stopped after he returned from his third trip.

Mother would smile and say, "Your father could have reached his goal had he had backing. But instead, you were born. Had you been a boy, you would have been his career. Do you wonder why he was so greatly disappointed upon your birth?"

I heard of my father's journeys to Seoul off and on from mother all through my childhood. I couldn't help but think of my father's dogged determination to succeed as well as my mother's persistence when I faced my most discouraging situations.

On that March night in Wesleyan, I wondered how I should approach my goal. What talent had I to use as a tool? An ability to speak was about the only tool I possessed. Fortunately, God confirmed that small talent at the S.V.M. Quadrennial Convention. Because of it, an unexpected opportunity was given me to speak in colleges for one year.

For years after that, I wondered if anyone had ever managed to start a school by speaking. I never heard of anyone until I went to Philadelphia to speak under the auspices of the Philadelphia Public School Board. The friend who was instrumental in getting these dates said, "Induk, I will take you to the administration building and show you the statue of Russell H. Conwell. You should see it because he founded Temple University by giving speeches."

She continued, "I hear you, too, want to start a school for your country's young men and women."

I stayed with this friend one week, speaking three times a day, twice in the morning and once in the afternoon, in different schools. One day my friend took me to see Conwell's statue. She told me how he had started his lecture on that famous topic, "Acres of Diamonds."

When I saw his statue, I quietly offered a one-sentence prayer: "God, do it again with me."

You may have heard the story. While Russell Conwell was touring ancient countries in the Middle East, he hired a camel driver as a guide. As he swayed along, the driver began to tell a story.

There lived an ancient Persian, Al Hafed, who owned a large farm with orchards, grain fields, and beautiful gardens. He was a contented and wealthy man—contented because he was wealthy, and wealthy because he was contented. One day a Buddhist priest called on him and told him how the world was made: mountains and hills, plants and minerals—silver, gold, and diamonds.

"A diamond is a congealed drop of sunlight," the priest told him. "It is the last and highest of God's mineral creations, as woman was the last and highest of God's animal creations."

(That might be the reason that women love diamonds, Russell Conwell said.)

The old priest concluded his story by telling Al

Hafed that if he had just a handful of diamonds, he could purchase anything he wanted, even the throne of a great country.

That night Al Hafed couldn't go to sleep because he didn't have a diamond mine for himself. Early next morning, he went to see the priest and asked him, "Will you tell me where I can find diamonds?"

The priest replied, "Diamonds? What do you want with diamonds? If you will find a river that runs over white sands, you will always see diamonds."

So Al Hafed sold his farm, left his family in charge of a neighbor, and went away to search for diamonds. He wandered through Persepolis and Palestine, and on into Europe. He used up all his money, became old and poor, weak and sick. In despair he took his own life.

Meanwhile, the man who bought Al Hafed's farm found diamonds in his own backyard where the brook was flowing. One morning when he led his camel to the clear brook to drink, he noticed a curious flash of light from the sands of the shallow stream. Reaching in, he pulled out a black stone which reflected all the colors of the rainbow. He took this curious stone into the house, left it on the mantle, and forgot all about it.

A few days later the same priest stopped at the farm. He rushed up to the mantle and said, "Here is a diamond. Has Al Hafed returned?"

The new owner said, "No, no, Al Hafed hasn't returned, and that is not a diamond. It is nothing but a stone."

But the priest persisted, "I know a diamond when I see one, and this is a diamond."

The two men rushed to the garden and stirred up the white sands with their fingers. They found other, more beautiful, more valuable diamonds than the first one. Thus the diamond mines of Golconda were discovered—the most magnificent diamond mines in all the history of mankind, exceeding the Kimberley in value. The great Kohinoor diamond in England's crown jewels and the largest diamond on earth in Russia's crown jewels came from that mine, the camel driver told Russell Conwell.

Russell Conwell utilized the old fable to help his enterprise. "Do what you can with what you have where you are today." He gave over 6000 speeches on this theme under the title "Acres of Diamonds" during his public life.

Dr. Conwell was a New Englander, a Yale graduate who joined Lincoln's army in 1861, rising from private to colonel. After the war, he became a foreign correspondent for the *New York Tribune* and the *Boston Traveler*. It was on one of his world tours that he heard the tale of the diamonds.

Dr. Conwell was a lawyer, too. When a man sought advice concerning the disposal of a bankrupt church in Lexington, Dr. Conwell took it as a personal challenge, became a minister, and renewed the life of the church. While serving there, a deacon from a struggling church in Philadelphia, Temple Baptist, heard him preach and asked him to come and help. Dr. Conwell accepted this new challenge in Philadelphia and put new spirit and hope into the church. One day a young man came to Dr. Conwell, expressing a desire to prepare for the ministry. Dr. Conwell offered to teach him one night a week and asked him to bring his friends.

On the appointed evening, seven earnest young men appeared. They were Dr. Conwell's "diamonds," from his home church. This group of young men were a nucleus of the future Temple University.

In Temple Baptist Church today, there is a pulpit in memory of the four World War II chaplains who gave their lifejackets to soldiers who didn't have any and went down together with a stricken ship. The pulpit was built with a special design to meet the needs of different forms of service—Protestant, Catholic, or Jewish. All one need do is turn the pulpit until he finds his own.

What a privilege it was to see Temple Baptist Church and Temple University! When I walked on the campus, I felt the presence of the great man who founded it. There my dedication was renewed and my commitment was strengthened.

I had my own dream about diamonds. It was not mere imagination but a real dream, that came while I was asleep. This was the second significant dream in my life. The first one I mentioned earlier—"Be a Missionary." That had to do with my personal life, but this second one was about a school.

In my dream, I went to a beach on the Han River. This is the river which flows through Seoul to the port of Inchon, twenty-five miles away, where it empties into the Yellow Sea. It was a spring day in my dream. I went to the Han River beach all by myself. There were some groups of children and young people enjoying games of ball on the white sandy beach quite a distance from me.

Even in my dream, I thought of the story "Acres of Diamonds." In my dream, I thought to myself, this is the place where one can find diamonds—a sandy beach. I dug into the white sand with my right hand, and lo and behold, I found three beautiful, sparkling diamonds. One appeared to be about one-half carat, another was a little larger, and the third a little smaller. In the sunlight, they were so brilliant with all the rainbow colors. Indeed, they were beautiful to behold!

In all the excitement, I wanted to find a much, much larger diamond, at least one carat in size, so I reached into the sand again. This time I found a bigger diamond, the size of my thumb. I held it up to the sunlight, but much to my disappointment there was no brilliancy. It looked dull and lifeless. Even in my dream, holding the uncut diamond in my hand, I asked God, "What is the matter with this diamond?"

The answer came, "It is a diamond in the rough.

You will have to polish it for a long, long time. But keep on polishing it until you get full brilliancy from it."

I woke up and realized it was a dream. I knew it was a vision given to me about "the school." It would take many, many years. "Yes, God, I will see it through with you."

There are many types of schools one could take for a pattern; but as for me, I had a definite idea what type of education Korean boys and girls, particularly boys, needed. It had to be an education using their hands and brains. By tradition, our boys are loathe to use their hands. With this idea firmly fixed in mind, I was looking for a school to be a pattern for the one I dreamed of starting. My travels with the S.V.M. gave me an opportunity to see many campuses.

One of the first colleges assigned to me was Berea College in Berea, Kentucky. I always inform myself before going to speak at a new place. Before going to Berea, three days before Thanksgiving in 1928, I briefed myself on that college.

It is unique in helping the young men and women from the Appalachian region. It has a splendid program of work and study, learn and earn. There are programs for farming, printing, arts and crafts, brick-making, baking, candy-making, and many other fields. I avidly read all I could find about Berea College. When I had finished, I said to myself, "God, this is it! Berea College is the pattern I should follow. How did you know I needed to go to Berea?"

As scheduled, I appeared on the platform of Berea College. The entire student body came to the convocation to hear me. Dr. William J. Hutchins introduced me and I spoke for about thirty minutes. I told them of my first Christmas when I got a No. 2 yellow pencil and pad, my experience in a boys' school masquerading as a boy, and my six months' imprisonment in solitary confinement under the Japanese occupation.

The students gave me a standing ovation such as I had never had before. As Dr. Hutchins escorted me from the floor, I asked him a very serious question. I said, "Dr. Hutchins, how can I start a school like yours in Korea under the Japanese occupation? We need one like Berea."

He seemed almost startled that such a serious question should come from a young woman. I still can see the expression on his face. He paused for a moment, then answered my question with a challenge.

"Why don't you start 'Berea in Korea'? You can do it. Where there is a will, there's a way."

"Berea in Korea?" Immediately, a ticking and clicking began in my mind. With much excitement I said, "Dr. Hutchins, that's a million-dollar phrase . . . Berea in Korea!"

I was glad then that I came from Korea, for Berea rhymes with Korea. After a little thought, I asked Dr. Hutchins what I could use as a springboard to launch such an idea in Korea. We have a saying at home, "Even an ox has to have a fence to rub its back on." I needed a fence to "rub on."

Dr. Hutchins replied emphatically, "Why not build a fence yourself with your No. 2 yellow pencil?"

Build a fence myself with my No. 2 yellow pencil! That was an idea! That meant I had to write. Write what? Write in English about my life? And so the idea began to take form in my mind—rather vaguely, for a long time. In the meantime, I was busy with speaking engagements.

I spent Thanksgiving with Dr. and Mrs. Hutchins. When I left Berea College the following Monday, I felt like a millionairess, minus the currency. That million dollars seemed very remote, but I felt that it could be obtained.

CHAPTER III

I didn't find my friends;
the good God gave them to me.
—Ralph Waldo Emerson

I am very rich in friends. Without them, Induk Vocational High School would never have been realized. They supported my dream of establishing "Berea in Korea"—confident that it would be realized some day.

One can understand when a friend supports a dream for one or two years, but ten, twenty, or more years, is hard to imagine. My dream took so long to reach fruition—thirty years! Some of my loyal supporters left this world before the school became a reality. I can vouch for their prayers at the throne of God. My mother is one of them. I can visualize how mother approached God on behalf of my dream: "God, will you please help Induk realize Berea in Korea soon?"

I can hear his answer: "I am not in a hurry, but I am always on time."

Actually, Berea in Korea opened twenty years after mother died. I know she prayed for all of those twenty years. When one is on earth, Christ lives in him. When he leaves this world, his soul lives in Christ.

One of my oldest friends is Mrs. Easter Lily Gates of Fort Lauderdale, Florida. I met her while I was speaking for the Florida Chain of Missions. A group of leading women from different denominations banded together to invite missionaries from both home and foreign fields to speak about their work. The idea started in the St. Petersburg area and soon became a chain throughout Florida.

I was first invited by the Florida Chain of Missions in January, 1931. I had never been to Florida before—God was opening a new territory for me. Where could I find a better place to meet friends from all over the United States and Canada than Florida in the winter?

After my first trip to St. Petersburg I went home to Korea, returning in 1936 to speak for the S.V.M. Quadrennial Convention in Indianapolis, Indiana, and for the Florida Chain of Missions. Meeting Easter Lily Gates was timely and significant. In the course of forty years of friendship, she has opened many doors for me—churches, women's clubs, and service organizations.

One of the reasons we became good friends was that our lives are parallel. The circumstances of her birth led to her unique name—it was given to her by her grandmother because she was born on Easter Sunday. In somewhat the same way, my father named me *Im-duk* (virtuous woman) to counteract my strong animal signs. I was born on the day of the dragon and the hour of the tiger in the year of the monkey and the month of the rooster.

My Confucian father placed great reliance in these signs. "She is a monkey, a rooster, a dragon, and a tiger," he said. "What if she shows all these natures—acting like a monkey, crowing like a rooster, powerful as a dragon, and raging like a tiger? A boy with these endowments might stir the world! It is too bad she is a girl!"

In Korea, a virtuous woman is quiet, obedient, gentle, and devoted. Meekness is not one of my characteristics, so I have kept all my life the name *Induk*—a boy's name meaning benevolence and virtue, which my mother gave me when she sent me to a boys' school. The difference may be subtle—but it is enough!

Easter Lily and I were both widows, with two children of about the same ages. From the Korean point of view, she had the edge on me because hers were sons and mine, daughters.

Easter Lily's hat is her trademark, as Korean dress is mine. She loves hats and always wears one when she goes out. Her favorite color is purple. When she appears in a purple dress, hat, shoes, and pocketbook, she looks stunning, almost regal. Above the striking outfit, she has a twinkle in her eye.

Neither of us likes to cook. Before she was married to George Gates, her mother told him, "You know she does not know how to cook or sew."

But George replied, "I'm not looking for a cook. I want a wife."

After their home was destroyed by a hurricane in 1926, her husband died, leaving her with two little boys. For a time she made a living by driving a school bus. Then she became supervisor of election registration, a position she held for forty years. If I happen to be in her home on Friday, she takes me to the Chamber of Commerce breakfast in Fort Lauderdale. The men, young and old, greet her enthusiastically, whistling and clapping. She is much loved wherever she goes—many consider her the landmark of Fort Lauderdale.

One year when I was to catch a bus to West Palm Beach, we had the wrong schedule and arrived at the station after the bus had pulled out. Easter Lily stepped on the gas. Her car was a "Wildcat," designed to make a warning noise when it went more than seventy-five miles an hour. Disregarding that, she drove the ten miles to Boca Raton in time to catch the bus there. No wonder she is known as "hot-rod sister."

Easter Lily is a staunch believer in God, always ready to lend a helping hand where there is need. Had it not been for her faith she could never have gone through the sorrows, sadness, and financial difficulties of her early widowed life. She reads the Bible and lives by it.

When Iris and her two boys came to America, I wanted them to meet Easter Lily. I knew she would welcome my family with open arms and give them food and shelter in her own home. But how could they get there? We did not have any means for such a trip. Whenever I need an idea, I pray. I just give myself up completely to the presence of God.

Here is the difference between Confucius's sayings and those of Jesus. Confucius said, "You do not live one hundred years, yet you worry enough for a thousand years." What a discouraging statement! No way out. Man born in this world lives in darkness, hopelessness, and dies.

But Jesus has given a wide-open door for life, now and forever. He said, "Come unto me, all who labor and are heavy-laden and I will give you rest. Take my yoke upon you, and learn from me; for I am gentle and lowly in heart, and you will find rest for your soul. For my yoke is easy and my burden is light."

And He said, "I am the way, the truth, and the life."

While I was contemplating a Florida trip for my family, a letter came from the Rev. Florence S. Stevens, Superintendent of the Methodist Deaconess Home in Providence, Rhode Island. She said she was going to Florida in August and asked me to join her.

Every time I encounter such unexpected situations, invariably and instinctively I say, "God, did you know it?"

And he replies, "Of course I did. Didn't you ask me for it?"

I wrote Miss Stevens by return mail that I had to be in Boca Raton ten days earlier, but that Iris and her boys would like to accompany her. Before I knew it, the trip for my family was all set.

When my family arrived in Fort Lauderdale, I was there to greet them. Easter Lily had to leave immediately for a week of official meetings in Tampa, but she gave Iris a purse with grocery money and the key to the house. We were both so moved we were speechless.

The next day was Saturday. Mr. and Mrs. Hamilton C. Forman, whom I met at the Boca Raton "Camp Farthest Out," invited us to go deep-sea fishing. I have known about ordinary fishing since the days when I went to a boys' school when I was seven, and did everything the boys did: running, climbing trees, quarreling, even skating and fishing—but not swimming!

We Koreans tell a fishing story about a man called Kang Tae-Kong who lived in China 120 years before Christ. Kang Tae-Kong was a politician and strategist during the Chu Kingdom. But he refused to use flattery or bribery to obtain a position in the government. Instead, he went fishing day in and day out, month after month, for years. He never used a hook—instead, a straight needle. Therefore, he never caught any fish, but he did a lot of meditating and waiting. News of Kang Tae-Kong and his fishing reached even the king. One day he was called into the king's court where he was recognized for his honesty, skill, and talent as a statesman. The king asked him to help his son, the crown prince, rule the country.

Of course, the most famous story in connection with fishing is in the Bible. When Jesus was passing along by the Sea of Galilee, he saw Simon and Andrew casting nets into the sea, for they were fishermen.

Jesus said to them, "Follow me and I will make you fishers of men." And immediately they left their nets and followed him. And going on a little farther, Jesus saw James the son of Zebedee and John his brother, who were in their boats mending their nets. And immediately he called them, and they left their father Zebedee in the boat with the hired servants and followed him.

Reading this story again from the Bible, two words stuck me like lightning—*follow* and *immediately*. I often wondered why Jesus chose those twelve men to be His disciples. Now I can understand. They were ready. Otherwise, they wouldn't have left immediately.

Deep-sea fishing would be a new experience for us and we were all eager to go! Iris was placed in the main seat, well-wrapped with strong leather belts so that if she hooked a big fish she would not be pulled into the sea. She held a rod with a long line and baited hook. Joong Hee, Sun Hee, and I each had a regular fishing rod with hook, line, and sinker. The men threw dead fish into the water around the boat to lure the fish.

Suddenly, Sun Hee, the younger boy, screamed, "I've caught a fish! I've caught a fish!" in Korean.

We were all excited and helped him pull in the fish. It was about five pounds.

A few minutes later, Joong Hee also screamed, "I've caught a fish! I've caught a fish!" We helped him pull in a beautiful fish, somewhat smaller than his brother's—about three pounds.

Both boys were happy because they had caught fish before either their mother or their grandmother. As if we were taking turns, I was the next to get a bite, and screamed just as excitedly as the boys had. Hamilton Forman came to my rescue. The line was so heavy that we thought the fish had to be at least ten or fifteen pounds, but it was nothing but a porous rock. Was I disappointed!

The big excitement was a little longer in coming. Iris held her rod for more than an hour before she felt a tug on the line. She fought the fish for half an hour before bringing it close enough for the men to get it on the boat, and had bruised arms for weeks afterward. I know she has tenacity and perseverance in whatever she does.

We took the big grouper back to the Florida Fishing Association to have it weighed and measured. It was one hundred twenty-three pounds, five pounds heavier than Iris herself, and was three inches longer than Iris's height of five feet, one and a half inches. Her name was registered as an expert fisherwoman. I was reminded of the old proverb, "Even a fish wouldn't get into trouble if it kept its mouth shut."

It was a wonderful experience for Iris to have caught such an enormous, edible fish from the Atlantic Ocean with the help of our Christian friends. The fish was divided into three parts: one-third was sent to the Rescue Mission, one-third was given to a friend, and one-third furnished food for the remainder of our stay in Florida.

We were all to return to Washington, D.C., by car with Miss Stevens. As we waited for her to pick us up very early one cool, breezy morning, my thoughts turned to Korea. Were it not for my American friends, my family might be refugees somewhere in Korea. They were refugees in Pusan during the Korean War, when little Sun Hee was only a few weeks old and Joong Hee was not quite three. Their father is among the many who are missing from that war, and their life in Pusan is hard to describe. It was a miracle that they survived! I was in America and could not help them. Now, nine years later we were all together, waiting for a friend to take us home to Washington. Another miracle!

On that return trip, there were seven in the car. Soon after we left Fort Lauderdale, it became very foggy. As usual, I prayed God to hold the wheel through Florence Stevens's hands. This is always my prayer when I board a train, bus, plane, or private car. Then I feel relaxed. I travel an average of one hundred to one hundred fifty miles a day, and have had no mishaps.

We decided to stop at Lake Wales to see the Bok Singing Tower. I had seen it a number of times, but Iris and her boys had not. It is the gift of Edward Bok to the American people. He came to America at the age of six from the Netherlands. The story goes that his father told him to make every place he went cleaner and more beautiful than it was when he arrived. Edward Bok became editor of the *Ladies' Home Journal.* He and the *Journal* worked for thirty years for such causes as the better babies movement, social hygiene, and beautification of American cities. Indeed, he left this world better than he found it. The Singing Tower is evidence of his philosophy.

The Tower is two hundred fifty feet high and stands in a fifty-acre park at Mountain Lake, near Lake Wales, Florida. It contains one of the largest carillons in the world. In the garden is a plaque with these words:

> The kiss of the sun for pardon,
> The song of the bird for mirth;
> You are nearer God's heart in a garden
> Than anywhere else on earth.

None of us talked while we walked in the garden. There was complete quiet and tranquility. I prayed, "God, what will be my gift to the American people?" I knew what it should be. My American friends do not expect a material gift from me. My gift should be producing many Edward Boks for Korea. By helping make Korea strong, I will help America to be strong. Eisenhower said, "Only strength can cooperate. Weakness can only beg." I wanted Iris and her boys to learn a living lesson from the Singing Tower excursion.

Two other Florida friends have helped me for many years. I met Mrs. Harvey W. Cotton of St. Petersburg through the Florida Chain of Missions, also. Originally from Maine, Ruth Cotton is active in the First Congregational Church, the Y.W.C.A., and other women's organizations in St. Petersburg. When I go there, I make my home with her. She is tall, slender, and efficient—and she always serves cooked oatmeal for breakfast, because she knows I love it!

Through Ruth Cotton, the Business Women's Club of the Y.W.C.A. became my loyal supporter. This club bought the first cow for Yang Kok, a village in Korea where I taught women and girls in the 1930s. Cows are very important to the farmers in Korea because they are used as beasts of burden as well as for breeding. Only a well-to-do farmer could be the sole owner of a cow. Others own one cooperatively. I thought it would be very helpful to poor Korean farmers if I could get some cows from different organizations in America. I called my project "Co-op Cows for Korea," and got quite a number. My American friends loved to name their cows—the Kappa Phi Club in Oxford, Ohio, called their's "Ox Ford" and the St. Petersburg Business Women's Club called their's "Business Women's Cow." Each year this club sends me a check to be used for our schools.

Ruth Cotton made me a life member of the St. Petersburg Y.W.C.A., so I feel as if I belong to St. Petersburg. I'm told their radio call letters WSUN stand for *W*hy *S*tay *U*p *N*orth. They also interpret the abbreviation for California as *C*ome *A*nd *L*ive *I*n *F*lorida. Being a foreigner learning to speak English, I love acronyms, phrases, idioms, and jokes. I understand that a foreigner really knows English when he understands the jokes, and I think I am doing quite well in that line because I am willing to learn.

Another long-standing friend is Martha H. Pangborn of Clearwater, Florida. I met her when she was living in Rye, New York, many years ago, and have been coming to her lovely home in Clearwater ever since she moved to Florida. It is one of the unusual blessings

God gave me to have her as my friend. She is meticulous, orderly, and artistic. Each year in January, she gives a tea for me, inviting my friends as well as hers. I know she plans these occasions prayerfully; for like Martha in the Bible, she is always busy working for her church and her friends.

In 1966, I took eight friends to the Orient. Our destination was our new school in Seoul. It was only three years old, and I wanted my friends to see it.

Martha Pangborn was one of the group. We were all to meet in San Francisco on July 30. The plane Martha was to take from Chicago was grounded by a strike, so she took the bus instead. As for me, I followed my usual mode of travel—Greyhound. When my bus stopped in Rock Springs, Wyoming, I went into the ladies' room and there was Martha Pangborn! After that, we met at every comfort stop until we reached San Francisco.

I have been to Honolulu many times on my journeys between America and Korea and have spoken there at "Camps Farthest Out" also. I made an unusual friend there, Helen Graff, then in her seventies. Her mind was always alert and she acted accordingly.

"I do not collect things, but I do collect friends," she told me. "I don't have to dust them." It has been twenty years since then, but her saying is a jewel I make good use of.

I feel strongly and positively that God brings people together when we are needed of each other. As Ralph Waldo Emerson said, "I didn't find my friends; the good God gave them to me."

Yes, I am rich, very rich, in friends whom God gave me.

CHAPTER IV

The three really great things in the world are a
mountain, an ocean, and an earnest man at his
work. The potentialities of each are beyond calculation.

—Edward Bok

Ever since I was six, the hills and mountains, rivers and
seas attracted my attention. I was born in the hamlet of
Monyangtul, three miles west of Port Chinnampo, now
in North Korea. A river flows between two ranges of
mountains and empties into the Yellow Sea. If I climbed
the hill in back of my home, I could see nothing but
water beyond the mountains.

The last sight I had of my birthplace was when I
was six years and seven months old. Yet I have a vivid
memory of it because it was an unusual last scene.

Mother had accepted Christianity in place of
Buddhism and decided to educate me in a private boys'
school in Duk Dong, seven miles from our village. Of
course, she had to disguise me as a boy. All the ar-
rangements were made with her distant relative Kim, a
Christian, who owned the school.

It was a clear, beautiful spring day when mother
and I left Monyangtul. The whole world looked fresh in
its green spring attire. Mother knew she couldn't inherit
my father's estate according to the old Korean way,
without a son. Since she had embraced the new Chris-

tian way, she relinquished all of her earthly possessions and ties with old customs and traditions. She uprooted herself from the old, non-Christian life, starting a new life as fresh as the spring. What a daring action she was taking—so calmly without any commotion.

Mother carried only a little bundle of clothing and, taking me by the hand, we left our thatched-roof house and walked along the narrow dirt road toward the hilltop, east of the village. Everyone, young and old, turned out to send us off. Some of the old women shed tears as they said their last farewell, "Go in peace."

Mother replied, "Stay in peace," and we proceeded on our way. Although more than seventy years have passed, I can still see their waving hands.

When we reached the top of the hill, we paused for a moment for a last glimpse of Monyangtul nestled down in the valley. I am sure mother must have had a million reminiscences, for she had lived there for a quarter of a century. But for me, the future beckoned! I saw a big steamer slowly navigating toward the west, its funnel belching smoke. I wondered where it was headed and wished I were on it. Later I learned that steamer could go to Japan, Shanghai, Hong Kong, Singapore—even to America.

While I was still gazing at the steamer, mother asked me to start going down the road. She said, "We have a long way to go today." Suddenly she started singing, "What a Friend We Have In Jesus." She had a naturally beautiful voice and perfect pitch. As I look back on that special day and spot, I cannot help but think that hilltop was mother's Continental Divide between the old life and the new. It was the beginning of a new chapter in her life. I never cease to thank God for her audacity.

It took me a long time to fulfill my wish to be on a steamer in the Pacific Ocean and to see the Continenal Divide at Pike's Peak. I had to pinch myself to see if I were really awake when I actually boarded the Dollar liner S.S. *Wilson* for my first trip to America.

I learned a lot about the ocean when I sailed on it for three weeks—two weeks from Yokohama to Honolulu and one week from Honolulu to San Francisco. My friend Inae Lee and I were in the steerage. Inae was going to America to be married and I, to be a student. The fare in steerage was $60 in those days. When we were taken down stairway after stairway, endlessly, I thought I was going to America through the center of the earth—I had heard that China and America face each other through land and water.

When we landed in the steerage, there were three tiers of berths around the room and one in the center. Fifteen berths were taken by Chinese, Japanese, and Filipino women. Inae and I were given one of the left-over tiers. Inae preferred the upper berth. The first two days we had fairly smooth sailing. We steerage passengers had our own deck at the stern of the steamer, roped off from the first-class passengers. We could climb up anytime we wanted.

During the two weeks it took to reach Hawaii, I found that the ocean has its moods and tempos like a person. Sometimes it was so calm that the surface looked like a vast mirror reflecting a deep blue sky, so still and serene. But sometimes it was stormy, violent, and treacherous, with surges of mountain-like waves. It got so angry that it seemed as if it might swallow up the whole ocean liner. The worst time was when the steamer was pushed up high and dropped down. I still can hear the sound of agony coming from those women, each in her own language. Some were just moaning. I still can see the portholes buried in the ocean. In the midst of the terrifying storm, I was comforted by what I had heard: the whole Pacific cannot sink a ship unless water gets into it. I knew the ship builders knew all about it when they built it.

I was the only passenger in the steerage who knew English. The steward brought me a booklet about the ocean. I read it avidly and learned a lot. The oceans which cover two-thirds of the earth's surface are very important in my life. Rainwater comes originally from the oceans; it sinks into the ground, feeds the streams, and returns to the oceans. The oceans are a source of food and minerals. Many scientists believe that many more sea products can be used as food to reduce hunger throughout the world. What a comforting thought! No wonder Edward Bok said that the potentiality of the ocean is beyond calculation.

Mountains, too, are full of special meaning for me. We know the value of mountains. Some have rich minerals, some forests, and some rushing streams and waterfalls which are harnessed to provide electric power, heat, and light. Many people of the world make their living by grazing animals on the grassy mountain slopes.

The mountains also inspire, challenge, and satisfy the spirit of adventure. When Sir Edmund Hillary of Australia climbed Mount Everest, the highest peak in the world, he was asked why he gambled with his life. His answer: "because it was there." The satisfaction of conquering great odds called him.

Great events have taken place on mountains. The Ten Commandments were given to Moses on Mount Sinai. The transfiguration of Jesus took place on a high mountain.

Of all the mountains I have seen in the United States, I have been most inspired by Franconia Notch in New Hampshire. It is where one can see the Old Man of the Mountains. I first went there in 1948 with Mrs. Howard W. Knight. I had read the story of "The Great Stone Face" by Nathanial Hawthorne while I was at school in Ewha, and had wanted to see it for a long time.

It was a beautiful May forenoon and white clouds

were playing hide and seek in the blue sky when Mildred Knight and I drove to Franconia Notch, but I could not see the face.

"Mildred, where is it?" I asked.

All she said was, "I will take you to the exact spot where you can see it. You cannot see it from any other place. I hope it won't be covered by clouds."

At last we reached the right spot. I looked up, and the white clouds were just unveiling the face. There it was! Both of us were silent. I thanked God for Mildred Knight's driving from Nashua so that I could see it. What a perfect face it is. It even has an Adam's apple. To me, the face resembles Abraham Lincoln's.

After watching it for several minutes, we returned to the car and drove on farther to see Indian Head. What puzzled me was this: the minute I moved away from that one spot, the face began to dissolve. I saw nothing but rocks, rocks, and more rocks—no face. This fact impressed upon me how important the right time and the right place can be.

When my daughter Iris Kim and her two little boys, Joong Hee and Sun Hee, came to America, we settled in a modest home in Washington, D.C. It has a big tulip tree which shades the whole backyard. Remembering my experience with the Great Stone Face—the importance of time and place—I start my morning devotions facing the tree when I am at home. I get ready for the day, and before starting my daily work I stand facing the tree, sing the Doxology, "Praise God from Whom All Blessings Flow," and repeat the Lord's Prayer. Then I sit on a chair and start my daily prayers, having the tree as my altar. I always feel God's presence more when I am in that position, time, and place.

Sometimes I picture Zacchaeus in that tulip tree and play his role. Imagination is one of the greatest gifts given to us. I read a story about Zacchaeus. From time to time, a friend noticed that Zacchaeus disappeared.

One day, out of curiosity, he followed his friend at a distance. Finally, Zacchaeus stopped at a sycamore tree and his friend came up to him.

"Zacchaeus, now I know where you go from time to time. But why?"

Zacchaeus answered, "Whenever I think of Jesus, I come over here, because I saw him from the top of this tree."

In 1950 when Korea was invaded by Communists from the north, Mildred Knight, then president of the New Hampshire State Women's Society of Christian Service of the Methodist church, invited me to speak in her state for two weeks. This was in September; the autumn foliage was so exquisite, so breathtaking, no matter where I went in New Hampshire. As I moved north to south, east to west in that state, I couldn't help but think of Korea. What could I do to help her be strong so that no one could attack her? Korea needs many earnest young men and women, strong and firm in purpose.

During that speaking tour, I spent a night with Mr. and Mrs. R. Howard Mitchell in Dover. Howard Mitchell was a very successful business executive, president of the Judson Dunaway Charitable Foundation. His wife Grace is most active in helping others. I met her mother, Mrs. Johnson, as well as her children and grandchildren, so I know four generations of the Mitchell family.

As the years passed, the Mitchells learned of the establishment of my first school, Induk Vocational High School. Mr. Mitchell wanted me to get to know Mr. S. Judson Dunaway, so he sent Mr. Dunaway a copy of my first book *September Monkey*. Mr. Dunaway read it and sent a contribution of $500 to our foundation.

Later I was invited to lunch by Mr. Dunaway at his home in Ogunquit, Maine, overlooking the Atlantic Ocean. His wife died a few years before I met him. My first impression was that he was a deadly earnest man with a definite purpose in life. From that time on, the

Mitchells and I have lunch with him once a year, either at his home or the Mitchells'. We got to know each other quite well, and he calls me "Lucky Ducky," because I told him that while in Wesleyan College I was called "Ducky."

Mr. Dunaway had a definite dream of helping others who were in need—an outgrowth of his childhood when he was a poor boy in Stanardsville, Virginia. His first job was as a janitor at his own school. Then he worked in his father's country store as a clerk, and learned the art of salesmanship. Later, when he was working and studying at the Y.M.C.A. in Philadelphia, his hero was Abraham Lincoln.

He started a corporation to manufacture Expello Moth Killer. But it was seasonal merchandise. Finally, after many trials and tribulations, failures and heartaches, he succeeded in manufacturing "Vanish," a product for all seasons and all homes. It is well-known in New England particularly.

In 1972, we built a workshop for Induk Vocational High School with funds partly donated by the Judson Dunaway Charitable Foundation, and named the building "The Dunaway Workshop." At present, 1800 boys in the last three years of high school are using that building, making things with their heads and hands. In 1976 we will have 2000 boys. Dunaway Workshop is the busiest building on the campus. It's like a beehive. We expect to produce many Dunaways for Korea who are as earnest as he was at his work.

Other friends I met on the same tour in New Hampshire were Mr. and Mrs. Wilfred J. King of Kittery, Maine. There is only a ridge between Kittery and Portsmouth, New Hampshire. My meeting with Wilfred and Ina King was pure serendipity! After an engagement at a church in Portsmouth, I was to return to Boston by bus. It was a rainy night in the fall. The Kings came to the church to hear me. By some misunderstanding, I was left without a ride. Right at that moment of my need, the Kings asked me, "Where do you go from here?"

"At this moment, I need to go to the bus depot here in Portsmouth," I answered, rather with relief. Without further ado, the Kings took me to the bus station.

Since then, I have been with them many times. Ina King offered to take me from place to place whenever I speak in that area. I am always grateful for that rainy night in Portsmouth when no one from the church showed up to take me to the bus station. God sent the Kings to rescue me. It was the beginning of my friendship with them.

Wilfred King was a mechanical engineer in the production department of the U.S. Naval Shipyard in Portsmouth. He designed special production equipment that was needed in the building of new submarines for the navy. His wife is a member of the Church of Jesus Christ of Latter-Day Saints. Until a Mormon church was built in their community, she was very active in the Methodist church.

The Kings live quite differently from most people in towns and cities. They have a large garden and raise all of their own vegetables; they even grow wheat, which they make into flour. Their chickens supply them with eggs.

Some years ago, I read the secret of a long, healthy life. First, one must have healthy parents. The offspring has no choice in this case. The second requirement is outdoor farm life, and the third, faith in God. The Kings have found the secret.

I never knew a Mormon personally until I met Ina. Since then, I have read many articles about them and have visited Salt Lake City. It is now the citadel of the Mormons, but when Brigham Young and his vanguard arrived in the valley in 1847, it was nothing but a wilderness. Only one tree grew on the spot. The thousands of trees that grow there now were all planted by Mormon settlers. They were so glad to find the soil good.

Brigham Young University was founded in 1875, twenty-eight years after the first Mormon settlement in what later became the state of Utah. Brigham called Dr. Karl G. Maeser to serve as principal and said, "I want you to remember that you ought not teach even the alphabet or the multiplication tables without the spirit of God."

On my first visit to Salt Lake City, I went to the Mormon Tabernacle and heard the famous Mormon Tabernacle Choir practicing. I couldn't help but think back a little over 100 years and picture the one lonely tree. What magnificent progress the Mormons have made!

Before being initiated into New Hampshire, the Granite State, I made many trips to Massachusetts. What a thrill and privilege it was to see Harvard, the first college in the United States, started in 1636, just sixteen years after the arrival of the *Mayflower*. I saw the history of the United States in miniature in the Boston area.

I often wonder why so many poets came from New England. To my Oriental mind, it must be because of the beauty of New England—fresh, fragrant, green in the spring with all kinds of flowers; in autumn, many different colors—from scarlet to rusty red, yellow to orange and brown, all blended into one exquisite color, covering the hills and dales, and high and low mountains. I am sure environment plays a very important role in one's life. We all know it and experience it.

We have a famous story of how the mother of Mencius, great philosopher of China, moved three times in order to give him a favorable environment. She lived first near a public cemetery. Little Mencius and his playmates imitated funeral processions all the time. Then she moved to a marketplace. This time her son and his friends imitated the people buying and selling goods and talked as they did. She knew that was not the place for her little Mencius to grow up. After much thinking, she moved near the school, and lo and behold, little Mencius learned to read and write, sitting cross-legged like the other boys.

With these thoughts in mind, I asked a friend, Henry F. Davis of Westwood, Massachusetts, why he thought New England produced so many poets. He said, "The early settlers were intellectuals with a Puritan heritage."

That was new light shed on the subject, but it reinforced my theory on beauty of the environment, rather than contradicted it.

I first met Mrs. Henry Davis at a church in Dedham, Massachusetts, many years ago. Mary is a thinking person; she and I speak the same language. She often invited me to meet with her international relations study group. When Mr. Davis was transferred to Charleston, South Carolina, Mary soon found a place in the work of Church Women United. She puts much skill and planning, prayer and hard work, into everything she does.

The Davis's son-in-law, Roger Flather, worked for the Peace Corps in Southeast Asia, then became active in an organization for famine relief, helping people to help themselves secure food, one of the three basic needs all men have: food, clothing, and shelter. I understand what it means to be hungry, for I experienced it when I was imprisoned in Westgate Prison, Seoul, under the Japanese occupation.

It is a constant wonder how God uses persons and occasions to open doors when I am in need. Through Mildred Knight, I made many speeches in New Hampshire. She also found engagements for me in Vermont. There I met Mary Catherine Root, a science teacher in a high school. One winter day I walked into her living room and saw the most beautiful rainbow colors shining before my eyes.

I asked "Mary Catherine, how did you capture the brilliant, vivid colors of the rainbow?"

She pointed to a crystal prism hanging near the window where the sun came in. I thought of what Henry Drummond said in his book *The Greatest Thing in the World:*

> As you have seen a man of science take a beam of light and pass it through a crystal prism, as you have seen it come out on the other side of the prism broken up into its component colours—red, and blue, and yellow, and violet, and orange, and all the colours of the rainbow—so Paul passes this thing, Love, through the magnificent prism of his inspired intellect, and it comes out on the other side broken up into its elements . . . Patience; kindness; generosity; humility; unselfishness; good temper; guilelessness; sincerity . . .

Following Mary Catherine's example, I have a crystal prism on the windowsill in my room in Washington, D.C., and whenever I see the rainbow colors I think of her as well as of Henry Drummond. There is the promise of God, implicit in this symbol of the rainbow—that He would not again flood the earth with forty days of rain as happened in the time of Noah (Genesis 9:8–18).

Mildred and Howard Knight "adopted" me as part of their family, and Mildred served as vice-president of our Berea in Korea Foundation until her death in 1972. She and her dauther, Ruth Robinson, would drive all the way to Washington, D.C., from Nashua, New Hampshire, more than five hundred miles in ice and snow, to attend our annual January board meetings.

Mildred and I discussed the possibility of helping worthy Korean young men and women come to America to get an education so that they could help Korea in the future. I had previously secured scholarships for friends' sons and daughters who had lost their homes and earthly possessions during the Korean War, acting as a "telephone operator" between the needy children in Korea and those friends here in America who were willing to help. By connecting two parties, I was able to help fifty boys and girls of high school age remain in school in Korea.

When I heard Mildred Knight's new idea—to bring college students to America—I knew it could be done. Mildred picked up the telephone directory and contacted colleges in New Hampshire. Colby Junior College of New London responded to our call and we set a date for an interview. This was the beginning of the project to get working aid scholarships. Since then, I have helped thirty-five young Korean men and women come to American colleges and universities with these scholarships.

Most of these students have returned to Korea to help our people with their particular specialization. I always told the students who came to America through the help of my friends to return to Korea and help the Korean people, because Korea needs them more than America does. That is the main reason we help them come for an education.

While I was speaking in Scranton, Pennsylvania, some years ago, Mrs. Braynard E. Kurkowski, a minister's wife, said to me, "Do you have any use for $500? Our United Church Women raised this amount for a Korean girl to come to Keystone Junior College in La Plume; but she didn't come. We would like to use the money for some other Korean young person."

I perked up and replied, "Could I use $500? I have a dear friend in Korea whose son, Hyung C. Chung, wants to come to America to study. This is an answer to my prayer." Chance favors those who are ready.

It was in November. Mrs. Kurkowski and I drove to Keystone Junior College and unfolded our plans to President Tewksbury. He arranged to send Hyung Chung all the necessary papers for him to get a Korean passport and visa. Hyung arrived the following autumn. The United Church Women of Scranton gave him $500, but he earned every penny of the rest, for he is a hard-working young man. I have heard that genius is one percent inspiration and ninety-nine percent perspiration. Hyung's father was founder of the Korean Boy Scouts. His oldest brother is now auditor for our Induk School Foundation in Seoul, and is working for the Boy Scouts in Korea, following in his father's footsteps.

How well Edward Bok said, "The potentiality of an earnest man at his work is beyond calculation."

CHAPTER V

Behold the turtle. He makes progress only when he sticks his neck out.

—Korean Proverb

We have our own creation story. First, a donkey was created. He asked the creator, "How long am I going to live, and what am I going to do?"

The creator answered, "You are going to live thirty years, carrying heavy loads for man."

The donkey said, "It's too long to do that. Just give me ten years."

The creator said, "You may have it."

Next, a dog was created. He asked the same question of the creator as the donkey. The creator said, "You are to live thirty years, watching over your master's home and barking at thieves."

The dog said, "I cannot do that for thirty years. Give me ten years."

The creator said, "You may have it."

Next, the monkey was created. He also asked the same question. The creator said, "You are to live thirty years, making faces and gibber-jabbering all the time."

The monkey said, "I cannot do that for thirty years. Just give me ten years."

The creator said, "You may have it."

Last, a man was created. He asked the creator, "How long am I going to live, and what am I going to do?"

The creator said, "You are going to live thirty years free—controlling the donkey, the dog, and the monkey. You will enjoy life and have a great time."

The man stuck his neck out and said, "That's too short a time. Give me some more years to enjoy life."

The creator was quiet for a moment, then said, "Well, I have some leftover years—twenty from the donkey, twenty from the dog, and twenty from the monkey. How about giving you sixty more years—ninety in all?"

By sticking his neck out, the man got sixty more years to live. The first thirty years are his own, with few obligations and responsibilities. From age thirty to fifty, he has to live a donkey's life bearing loads for this family, community, and country. From age fifty to seventy, he must live a dog's life, taking care of yards, making cookies for grandchildren, and babysitting. Finally, from age seventy to ninety, he has to live a monkey's life, making faces and gibber-jabbering all the time!

I am glad the man gained sixty extra years by being courageous. What kind of life would it be without those different stages?

The turtle is one of the ten Oriental symbols of longevity. The others are cloud, crane, bamboo, pine, mountain, water, ginseng, sun, and deer. In Korea, when a young man and woman are engaged to be married, the bride-to-be embroiders pads with the ten symbols and attaches them to both sides of a pillow for decoration. The front of the groom's wedding gown also has these ten symbols embroidered with pearls.

Ginseng has been known as the herb that serves as an elixer of life. Many, many centuries ago, Jin See, emperor of China, heard of this herb and sent 500 young couples to Korea to bring back ginseng roots. But they all chose to remain in Korea, and the emperor waited in vain for their return.

Whenever I think of a turtle's sticking his neck out, the word "courage" comes to my mind. I found the following lines by Edgar A. Guest:

> Courage isn't a brilliant dash,
> A daring deed in a moment's flash;
> It isn't an instantaneous thing
> Born of despair with a sudden spring.
> But it's something deep in the soul of man
> That is working always to serve some plan.

The best example I know of this kind of courage is the founding of the first school for girls in Korea by Mrs. Mary Scranton, in 1886. It was her plan to serve Korea and its people. Before she arrived, she studied carefully all aspects of Korea—its location; its people and their needs; and its political, economic, and spiritual characteristics. She learned that Korea was in a strategic location, surrounded by three powerful countries—China, 120 miles west; Japan, about the same distance east; and Russia, then possessing a twelve-mile borderline with Korea.

Korea, a peninsula no larger than the New England states plus New York and New Jersey, has something her neighbors need. To Japan, Korea can serve as a land bridge, a transition zone, and a buffer state between herself and China and Russia. To China, Korea serves as a buffer state between herself and Japan. For this reason Imperial China had insisted that Korea must remain independent.

To Russia, Korea is even more important. Despite possessing one-sixth of the world's territory, Russia does not have an ice-free port on the Pacific. She is a land-locked country and is most anxious to secure Korea's matchless seacoast with harbors facing in three directions. She has desired Korea since the days of the czars.

Mrs. Scranton knew Korea could not play her role politically, economically, and spiritually with men alone. She would need the assistance of her women, as a carriage needs two wheels. Mrs. Scranton conceived the daring idea of starting a school for girls and teaching them the love of God. Thus the birth of Ewha was her powerful weapon for Korea's strategy. What a significant, daring action she took! It was prophetic! Had she not stuck her neck out and moved to establish a school, where would I be today? What a tremendous impact her courage has made on me!

But the opposition made by some men at that particular time was like a fierce tiger poised and ready to spring. From a Korean man's point of view, schools for girls were unneeded. Every Korean home served in that capacity—with grandmothers, mothers, and aunts as teachers. Korean girls learned to be patient, kind, and loyal. Girls should not be heard or seen. Fathers argued, "Why do our daughters need anything more?"

Under such strict practices at home for centuries, our Korean women have been kept very much in the background and were not given an opportunity to participate in public or civic affairs. We had no voice. Korea had only stag parties for a long time until Christianity and women's education were introduced. To my way of thinking, stag parties lead only to stagnation.

It will be ninety years in 1976 since Ewha was founded by Mrs. Scranton out of her compassion and courage. As she had envisioned and foreseen, Ewha became the mother of all the other denominational mission schools for girls. As a women's college, Ewha became and has remained "Number 1."

I graduated alone in the third class of Ewha College. In the first graduating class were Marcella Syn, Alice Kim, and Dorothy Yi. All have made history in women's higher education in Korea.

Dorothy Yi married into the Jhung family and has four daughters. The remarkable fact is that all four graduated from the University of Michigan with honors. One is a medical doctor, one a geologist and meteorologist, one a chemist, and one a pharmacist. The Jhungs worked hard to give their daughters the best education possible. Above all, they are ardent Christians who practice their religion every day. Dorothy discovered this great source of power while she was in Ewha.

During my second year in Ewha College, Korea's first women's quartette was formed. Since the senior class had only three members, I was recruited to complete the quartette: Dorothy Yi, tenor; Alice Kim, soprano; Marcella Syn, bass; and myself, alto. We practiced a number of songs from the hymnal, but our favorite was "Rock of Ages." At first, we sang in our own Ewha Chapel and in our church, the First Methodist Church. As the news spread, we were invited to sing in other churches. The climax came when we sang at the Y.M.C.A. auditorium for 800 men. What a thrill we had deep in our hearts! It was quite daring for us to appear on the stage.

While we were studying Western music at Ewha, we learned that the first musician was Jubal. He was the father of all who play the lyre and pipe, and the inventor of the harp. Tubal-cain opened the first foundry, forging instruments of bronze and iron (Genesis 4:21–22).

We Koreans have sixty-five different musical instruments, starting with drums and gongs, oboes and flutes. The sounds of our music come from five different sources: metal, wood, water, fire, and earth. We have only five tones—do, re, mi, so, la—and a three- or six-beat system. Our best songs sound like spirited waltzes. Undoubtedly, Korean music is the only Asian music comparable in its richness and emotional complexity with the best of European music.

62

Korean dances are free, too, expressing the joy of life in billowy costumes, unlike the mysticism of Indian dance or the iron skill of the Japanese form.

In December, 1950, the half-destroyed city of Seoul was about to be captured by the Communists for the second time. Only a few hours remained to salvage precious national treasures, and our government ship stood by for one last-minute cargo. What could be evacuated that would be of most value to the nation? Machinery? Engraved plates for printing money? No, not any of those. Our government chose to rescue the Seoul Symphony Orchestra, for without music there could be no Korea. A singing people never dies.

When Iris graduated from Ewha Women's College in music, suddenly a historic honor was thrust upon us. We became the first mother-daughter college graduates in Korea's history. I said in my prayer, "Why, God?"

The quiet answer came through the Bible. "Everyone to whom much is given, of him will much be required" (Luke 12:48, RSV). I was startled when I read the phrase "of him will much be required." What a tremendous challenge it is! I felt challenged like young David.

Of all the battle scenes I have read or heard about, to me the meeting of young David and the giant Goliath is the most exciting. David picked up five smooth stones from a stream, put them into his shepherd's bag, and, armed only with his shepherd's staff and sling, set out to meet Goliath.

David shouted to Goliath, "you come to me with a sword and a spear, but I come to you in the name of the Lord of the armies of heaven and of Israel—the very God whom you have defied."

As Goliath approached, David ran out to meet him. Reaching into his shepherd's bag, he took out a stone, hurled it from his sling, and hit the Philistine in the forehead. The stone sank in and the man fell on his face to the ground. It was centrifugal force in a hurtling stone that killed Goliath. But it was courage that enabled David to face the champion of the Philistines in the first place. If we are bold enough, even the laws of motion will come to our aid. So David won the victory with a stone and a sling, with one motion. What are the five smooth stones? Miss Estelle C. Carver, my spiritual mentor, said, "The five smooth stones are: God is, God has, God does, God can, God will."

I realize that Korea has many Goliaths surrounding her. They appear to be formidable, unconquerable, and aggressive. We are challenged like David, but we have five smooth stones and a sling. What would take the place of a sling? A united front of our Korean women, organized to meet the challenge. We learned the method and technique from the American women. One woman is helpful, one hundred women are forceful, one thousand women are powerful, one million women are invincible! It seems that almost every American woman is involved in a church organization or a club. I discovered that the common denominator of all these organizations is service for church, community, nation, and the world.

The first organizations for Korean women were the Y.W.C.A. and the W.C.T.U. I heard a man interpreting W.C.T.U. as "Women Can Tell You." It sounded quite authoritative. In a sense, it is. The Korean W.C.T.U. is organized locally and nationally, and is also a member of the World W.C.T.U.

Following its purpose, the national Korean W.C.T.U. proved its power during the first national election. Korea was to elect the first president of the Republic of Korea after we were liberated by the Allied Forces from Japanese occupation. We sent a delegation to General John R. Hodge, commanding general of the Twenty-fourth Corps of the U.S. Army in South Korea, asking him to issue a special edict to close all the liquor stores and bars during the national election period so that our men could vote with clear minds. General Hodge complied with our requests. It was our first experience in dealing with such grave and serious national issues. With this exciting, workable plan as a united W.C.T.U. of Korea, we individual members felt great and important. At long last we found a secret weapon, five smooth stones and one sling. Our centrifugal force will be released when it is needed.

We Korean women helped our men to vote with clear minds and sobriety, and we voted too. It was the proudest moment when each eligible woman went to the polls and cast the vote for the candidate whom she chose without being told for whom to vote. It was the first time she had voted in Korea's long history. She helped set up the new democratic government—the Republic of Korea. We are united to lead our country forward.

Today in Korea, we have business and professional women and women in politics—teachers, doctors, nurses, and social service workers. Many of the restaurants and most of the tea rooms are managed by women. In Korea, a tea room serves an important function, because few homes have parlors in which to meet one's friends. Men go to the tea room to transact business in a social atmosphere—if they keep ordering tea, they may stay as long as they like.

The beauty parlors are run by women and we have women barbers. Women own tailor shops. Although there are no women bankers, a great many private loans are negotiated. We even have a woman contractor. One of the largest textile mills is managed by a woman. Another took over the presidency of the Newspaper Alliance when her husband died. What daring steps our women take!

Youth and bravery go hand in hand. There is no inertia in youth. They always ask, "What's new?" The young are energetic and adventurous. On the other hand, the old have experience, are mellow and wise.

I admire the American young people who form the Youth Temperance Council (Y.T.C.) for their courage and determination. They are not afraid like the man who received only one talent and buried it. They are resolved to stay cool and sober and help other youth remain that way, too. What commitment they have!

The Y.T.C. is helping the youth of other lands to live a committed life also. I have spoken at national and state conventions of the W.C.T.U. many times, and during the convention they always devote one evening to the Y.T.C. When I told the young delegates of my dream of starting Berea in Korea, they caught the vision and as a group raised $600 to help the project. I used it to buy additional property for our school. Now the Y.T.C. has a part in our school and we are part of them—together we will move ahead.

Many times I have been with the younger generation in America, speaking in churches, schools, camps, and conferences all over the United States, and have had intimate contact through my two grandsons who lived with me during their elementary and high school years. Each new generation reacts to the previous generation. If the older is conservative, the new is liberal and vice versa. As expressions of revolt against the older generation, the younger starts its own new outfits and hairdos, new plays and music, new eating habits, new ways of courtship, new patterns of belief and philosophy—these are the daring gestures of youth. They are ambitious dreamers, resilient in their thinking. They want to take the wheel of history into their own hands. Through experience they will mature in their own good time as each past generation has.

Give the young a hero and they will follow him. I have experienced it many a time. Will I ever forget how the young people reacted when young John F. Kennedy became president? "Ask not what your country can do for you. Ask what you can do for your country." The message was exhilarating and stimulating. His Peace Corps program caught the vision and imagination of many young men and women.

Ralph Waldo Emerson said that some of the youth know that one who surrenders himself to a great ideal himself becomes great! The soul that laughs and loves and rides for the right has all the world at his feet. We can name hundreds of men and women who have followed Emerson's advice and brought great achievements into this world for humanity.

In spite of all the changes taking place in each generation, the great values of life remain forever. The expression and tempo might be a little different, but the ideals and truth are fundamentally the same. A few years ago, I heard Fred Waring's performance in Little Rock, Arkansas. Although he had been performing for many years, he still seemed young and agile. His program was divided into three parts: past, present, and future. I waited for the third part, thinking he might present a song which had never yet been sung or played. Much to my surprise, one of the "future" numbers was "The Hallelujah Chorus." I realized then that anything which has eternal value is good for all ages and forever. No one can deny cause and effect. The seasons change; the sun rises and sets each day. There is no stop sign for time.

In my travels, I have discovered that the young people in the smaller city churches are quite different from those in big cities. One area with which I am quite familiar is the Pennsylvania Dutch country. The people are rather conservative, slow to change, holding to their own customs and culture. They are dependable, loyal, and devout. Their young people are more or less reserved. In Sunday Schools and young people's meetings, they read the Bible, pray aloud, and even testify to what they think in relation to life and religion, doubts and

67

hopes. They ask perceptive questions about life in Korea.

But what surprises me is the way these young people memorize Bible verses, verse after verse, by heart. Memorizing, to me, is the best exercise for brains. A friend of mine said, "If you don't want to become senile, memorize Bible verses, good hymns, and poems." I memorized the entire Gospel of Mark (without the genealogy) when I was in grammar school in Korea. Lately, I have memorized all forty verses of the eleventh chapter of Hebrews in English, and "One Solitary Life." I keep on memorizing. We have an old proverb: "Knife gets dull when used, but brain gets sharper when used."

With memorization, stimulation, and imagination, one's mind stretches and gets new ideas. A man like Thomas Edison, inventor of the electric light, stretched his imagination and mind, and accomplished much for society. Edison once said, "I have been able to discover many marvelous secrets of science and put them into my inventions; but some day, some fool is going to discover the power of prayer. His discovery will be greater than mine."

What a challenge!

CHAPTER VI

Many drops make a shower.
—Korean Proverb

When I definitely decided to start Berea in Korea, I knew it would take substantial funds, which I did not have. I thought about F. W. Woolworth's, where my yellow pencil No. 2 came from. It was a five and ten cent store; and without nickels and dimes, a dollar can't be made!

My next-door neighbor also reminded me that dollars would come if I looked after the nickels and dimes. William G. Hughes and his family moved to their present home just about two years before we came. They have been the most generous and helpful friends for all of the years we have been neighbors. Their two sons and Iris's boys grew up together.

Soon after we moved in, I saw Mr. Hughes building an additional room on their house. I found out that, although he was a communications specialist for the government, he was also a carpenter, an electrician, and a plumber. I asked him where he was graduated.

"UHK," he said.

I asked, "What university is that?"

The University of Hard Knocks," he replied. He can do anything, using his head, hands, and heart—creating new or making useless things into useful ones.

Mr. Hughes told me, "If you have a problem in electricity or plumbing, let me come and see it first. If I can't fix it, I'll tell you who can."

Indeed, he helped us more than words can tell. He saved us much money the first year after we moved in. To express our gratitude, I sent him a small check. Immediately, he came to our home and returned the check, saying that he tries to do what the Bible says.

"We must help widows and the fatherless when they are in need," he said. "I hear both you and your daughter are widows, and your two little grandsons are without a father. I should help you. If I didn't share my talents with you, God wouldn't like it."

Over a period of eighteen years, the Hugheses have been the most helpful and thoughtful of neighbors. The good God gave them to me.

The importance of making nickels and dimes is accentuated by what Harry Emerson Fosdick said about a dollar:

> A dollar is a miraculous thing. It is a man's personal energy reduced to portable form and endowed with powers the man himself does not possess. It can go where he cannot; speak language he cannot speak; lift burdens he cannot touch with his fingers; save lives with which he cannot directly deal . . . so that a man busy all day downtown can at the same time be working in boy's clubs, hospitals, settlements, children's centers all over the city.

What a miraculous thing it would be when the dollars worked for my young people through Berea in Korea! With this vision in mind, I was after that dollar, following Russell Conwell's method—making speeches. Conwell's topic was "Acres of Diamonds"—mine was "My Country and My People."

From that time on for many years, I did nothing but travel and speak. I would say I wore blinders always, so that I could see ahead only my goal in life—Berea in Korea. Getting speaking dates was no problem. When I was invited to speak at a conference or a local church or women's club, I always got three or four more dates from the women who heard me. It was like a snowball. I do not have a booking agent; my friends are my agents!

As for traveling, I usually choose the most inexpensive way. I noticed that by adding a few dollars to a one-way plane ticket, I could make a round trip by bus. Of course, it takes longer but for me Greyhound is my home away from home. I spend a night or two a week on the bus during the height of my speaking season every year. Instead of getting off the bus and spending the night in a hotel, I utilize the bus as a hotel, too.

I learn many interesting things on the bus. It has its own life-style and philosophy. My favorite spot is the aisle seat just across from the driver. From this seat I can see where I am going with no obstruction. No extra charge. All one need do is get there ahead of any other passenger, stand in line as number one, and wait.

Quite often, I see a man and woman sitting together on the bus. They are strangers when the journey starts, but they start talking. At the next station, one gets off and another stranger comes in and sits beside the one who remains. Some people travel alone all the way to their destinations. Such scenes on the bus made me think: isn't marriage like that? When one loses a mate, a remarriage may take place; but some remain alone all their lives.

I once heard a very descriptive marriage definition: "Marriage resembles a pair of shears, so joined that they cannot be separated; often moving in opposite directions, but always punishing anyone who comes between them."

Some bus drivers are witty, unwittingly. While traveling through Illinois, I once noticed that the name of a town we passed through was Arcola and the next was Tuscola. To be facetious, I said to the driver, "Is the next town Coca-Cola?"

"No, it's Champaign," he replied.

One day on the bus I decided to write down all the warning signs along the road. I collected more than sixty—from "Slippery When Wet" to "You May Be Right But You May Be Dead Right." Advertising signs attracted my attention, too. In selling anything, I have learned a good slogan helps a lot. This is particularly true in the United States where people live in high gear—at high speed.

A slogan should be sharp and snappy, but full of meat and meaning. One of the best is Frank Laubach's famous slogan "Each one, teach one."

Rhyming slogans are easy to remember and fun to repeat. I think that's why people like mine: "Berea in Korea."

Many times buses are late because of the weather. During such times, I go through many exasperating and anxious hours; I have no power, absolutely none, to ease the situation. All I do is just pray. I have offered more prayers on buses than anywhere else. However, I have not missed one single date so far.

I want to give one illustration. I was to address the Women's Club in Washington, Connecticut. This date was made six months ahead of time. It had snowed heavily the previous day while I was still in Providence, Rhode Island; and consequently, the schools were closed, public meetings had been cancelled, and transportation was quite generally disrupted. However, I telephoned Washington, asked whether there was still to be a meeting, and received an affirmative reply. They asked how I planned to reach their town for there were no buses or trains directly to Washington. They advised me to go by way of Waterbury which was only twenty-three miles away. I looked up the train schedule and reported that I would be arriving in Waterbury at 1:00 P.M. The meeting was scheduled for 4:00 P.M.

I started out an hour ahead of time from the Deaconess Home where I had spent the night. I tried to get a cab but none was available. Then I waited for a bus to the station, but learned that it didn't go that far. Nevertheless, I boarded the bus and rode as far as I could, walking the remainder of the way. By the time I arrived at the station, I was fifteen minutes late; but since the train was coming from Boston, I assumed it wouldn't be on time, either.

When I arrived at the station, the stationmaster was calling out, "The New York train is arriving." I knew it would. My next problem was the train connection in Bridgeport for Waterbury. The timetable showed that I would have fifteen minutes to change from one train to the other, from the same platform.

I boarded the New York train; it stopped first in New Haven, then in Bridgeport. I rushed out and looked around . . . no connecting train. I asked the man at the station whether the train to Waterbury had left. He said that it had, a few minutes before. Well, I was in a dilemma—I could either wait for the next train which would be much too late for me to make the meeting in time, or I could hunt up the bus station and try my luck there. I was doing all this in prayer. The bus station was two long blocks away, but I lugged my heavy suitcase along. When I got there, a bus was ready to depart. I shouted to the driver; he heard me and opened the door.

He asked, "Where are you going?"

"Waterbury, Connecticut," I said.

He told me to come aboard, but I had to tell him I didn't have a ticket and would have to buy one.

"Oh, all right . . . I'm five minutes late already, but what does it matter on a day like this?"

What a happy-go-lucky disposition he had. It rather reminded me of our quaint saying, "My grandfather never hurried; my father never hurried; why should I hurry?"

It took only a few minutes to secure my ticket, and I hurried aboard and thanked the driver for waiting. I then asked how long it would take to get to Waterbury. When he told me one hour, my heart sank. It was then 12:30 P.M. Someone was expecting to meet me at 1:00 P.M. at the railroad station. There were many stops along the way, for the bus was local. I was becoming quite apprehensive.

The bus finally arrived in Waterbury at 2:30 P.M. I was an hour and thirty minutes late for my meeting with the lady from Washington. Thinking she must have returned home, I telephoned her house. A child answered. I asked where his mother had gone, and he replied in a sweet voice, "Mama's gone to meet a Korean lady."

I told him I would be waiting for her at the railroad station in Waterbury. I couldn't locate a taxi, so I walked five long blocks up the hill with my dressing case. Just as I was crossing the street to the depot, a young woman, looking around once more to see if a Korean lady was in sight before leaving for home, spotted me, rushed up, took my case, and said, "You are Mrs. Pahk, aren't you? Let's hurry! We have twenty-three miles to go and the road is very bad. The meeting is scheduled for 4:00, and we have just about an hour to make it. I'll tell you a strange story—why I waited for you for two hours."

Once in the car and on the way, my hostess explained that she had arrived at the station a few minutes ahead of time. She waited and waited, but no train came. She asked at the ticket window about the schedule and was told that the train was delayed by the bad weather. That was logical, so she waited another half-hour. Still no train. Becoming impatient, she asked again what the situation was, and the agent admitted that he was sorry, but he had previously given her incorrect information. The train referred to had been taken off after a terrible flood a year before. It would not come at all.

She said, "Had he not given me the wrong information, you would indeed be stranded, or I would have had to make another trip."

It was a blessing in disguise. "God works in a mysterious way His wonders to perform!" We arrived in Washington on time and the women were all waiting for us.

So far, I have spent more time traveling than staying in one place. During my travels I have had to wait hours and hours. If I counted all the time spent waiting over a period of many years, it would add up to several months. Of course, my most dreadful experience in waiting was the five months I spent in solitary confinement in Westgate Prison, Seoul, during the Korean Independence Movement. It was almost intolerable because I was young and couldn't see the end in view. I had no alternative but to sit and sit, waiting endlessly with what patience I could muster. As I look back on those months, it seems that I was preparing myself to wait for buses.

One day while waiting on the bus, a long-dormant thought popped out—"How about *September Monkey,* the book you are going to write?" I was really startled when the thought came to me. But I knew that the idea of writing *September Monkey* was about ripe and needed action. It was like a plant bulb that lies dormant during the cold winter, ready to burst out when spring comes. I knew when my book was published, getting funds to build Berea in Korea would be easier. Thus far, funds came only through my speaking.

Right away, I went to the lovely farmhouse in Salem, New Jersey, home of my friend Mrs. Mary DuBois, and started writing the book with her assistance. Then I took my rough copy to another friend, Mrs. William F. Becker, in Oak Tree, New Jersey. She revised it into a presentable manuscript. Anna Becker has a flair for writing. She knows the right words, phrases, and sentences to express thoughts.

The next problem was finding a publisher, and it seemed almost impossible because to begin with I was not a writer; in addition, I was a foreigner and a woman. A friend scared me by telling that her manuscript had been rejected by fourteen different publishers before it was accepted on the fifteenth try.

Luckily, this did not happen to me. I was introduced to Eugene Exman, editor-manager of the Religious Books Department of Harper and Brothers, by Weyman C. Huckabee, who had scheduled me to speak in different colleges and universities when I was traveling secretary of the Student Volunteer Movement. Mr. Exman accepted the manuscript, and one year later, on September 24, 1954, I was given the first copy of *September Monkey*. Only God knew how I felt when I actually had a copy in my hand. It was a miracle! That night at the home of my friend, Velma Van Court, sister of **Anna Becker, I dedicated** *September Monkey* **to God and to Berea in Korea.**

My book was reviewed in *The New York Times* Book Review section, and the first edition of 5000 copies was sold out in three weeks! No wonder writers want the *Times* to review their books!

Because of the unusual title of my book, I came in for some amusing incidents. When I spoke at St. Mark's Methodist Church in Brookline, Massachusetts, one Sunday, I was introduced in the bulletin as the author of *September Donkey*. The morning service was exceptionally well attended that day, and I noticed many in the congregation looking at me with broad smiles. I smiled back. After the service was over, I turned to the minister and corrected the error.

He said with a smile, "I don't know which one I prefer, a donkey or a monkey. If it is a donkey, I can ride it; but if it is a monkey I'll have to carry it. Whether it's a donkey or a monkey, it's a fascinating title." (Coincidentally, the foundation secretary, Lily, is a "September Donkey.")

While speaking at the women's missionary meeting of a church in Ohio, the minister introduced me as the author of *September Morn*. Everyone laughed except me. I didn't understand why the audience was roaring. When I stood up, of course, I corrected the title. After I had finished speaking, a most considerate lady approached me and said, "Haven't you seen a picture of 'September Morn'?"

I answered that I had not, and she immediately offered to send me one. She kept her word; and when I looked at it, I murmured aloud, "No wonder everyone in that congregation roared with laughter!" (The subject is a demure nude.)

Out on the West Coast, a friend of mine wrote me a very interesting reaction brought to her attention because of my book. Her daughter was a librarian in a large town in California. One day a woman walked into the reading room and asked for a copy of *Korean Monkey*. The librarian said she did not have a copy of *Korean Monkey*, but she did have a copy of *September Monkey*, written by a Korean woman.

The lady impatiently answered, "It doesn't matter whether it's a Korean Monkey or a September Monkey as long as it's the monkey story. I just loved it!" She signed her name and took out a copy of the book.

Soon after the publication of *September Monkey*, it was published by Gollancz in London, thus introducing me to the United Kingdom—England, Ireland, Scotland, Wales, Australia, New Zealand, and South Africa. Next, my book was translated into German and two editions were published by Vandenhoeck and Ruprecht in Gottingen. It was also translated into Norwegian and published in that country.

Perhaps the most heart-warming news was the fact that my book came out in Braille for the benefit of blind people. I was very moved by this news because of my dear blind friend, Mr. C. G. Steinhart, who gave me a scholarship when I was a student at Ewha.

When the publication of *September Monkey* became a reality, my dream of founding Berea in Korea was within reach. I had built a springboard to launch my project with a yellow pencil No. 2, and set it firmly on the ground in America. American people are genuinely interested in projects such as mine—helping other people help themselves. Furthermore, America is a land of opportunity and plenty. All I needed now was to work harder and pray more.

My next step was to get a permanent visa. Thus far, I had a temporary visa, renewable for six months at a time. The Immigration Office had been very sympathetic and lenient with me because of my work. One day I was led to Congressman James C. Davis of Atlanta, Georgia, who is married to my Wesleyan College classmate, Mary Lou Martin. He introduced Private Bill No. 2954 during the Eighty-fourth Congress. It was passed unanimously by the House and Senate, and a permanent visa was granted to me. Literally many, many friends prayed and wrote to their respective congressmen and senators on my behalf.

How did I feel when the telegram came from Congressman Davis about my permanent visa? I felt so great and so grateful that I could even jump the North Sea with a mountain under each arm, praising God so that the whole world could hear! I prayed that I would start Berea in Korea and let the whole world hear about it. Now I am in possession of a little green card, three and one-half by two inches. It is the most powerful card I have ever had. I can go anywhere in the world and still return to America as long as I possess that little green card.

Did I want it just for my own sake and benefit? God forbid! My purpose in obtaining it was to enable me to carry on my work to the aid and betterment of conditions for Koreans through Berea in Korea.

Soon after I obtained the permanent visa, I asked

Mr. David Carliner, a brilliant lawyer of Washington, D.C., to set up the Berea in Korea Foundation with a tax-exempt privilege from the Internal Revenue Service. It took one year for him to get this privilege. I am indebted greatly to his wisdom and effort. Before selecting the five members of the Board of Directors, I sought God's guidance. In a venture so wide in scope, so serious in import, I wouldn't dare proceed without his approval.

With my permanent visa and tax-exempt foundation, my *September Monkey* and I started traveling and speaking in full steam and full force for Berea in Korea.

From the time of my spiritual rebirth, I have not named a fee for my speeches. When I speak for church organizations, I am given a love offering, but women's clubs usually have a set amount for a speaker, as a matter of policy.

I had a rather unusual experience at the Women's Club in Hamburg, Pennsylvania, where I got more than I would ordinarily have received. A friend telephoned to ask if I would be free to speak at the women's club on November 3. "It is short notice, I realize, but if you are free, it would be a great treat for them," she said.

I went in the rain to that meeting in Hamburg and found it was the club's Twenty-fifth Anniversary celebration. They had planned an elaborate affair—a smorgasbord spread and a Spanish dancer to entertain. Three days before the event, the dancer broke her ankle and had to cancel her appearance; consequently, the club had to get a substitute. We can all appreciate how upsetting it is to be chairman when a main event in the program has to be changed.

In the midst of much confusion, I walked in. The president greeted me with a sigh of relief. She told me how glad she was to see me and escorted me to the speaker's table. There were 167 women present—a garden of human flowers awash with lively chatter and laughter.

After we were seated, the president turned to me and said in a despairing manner. "Somehow, things just won't go right for this celebration! First, the Spanish dancer had to disappoint us, and you are here in her place."

I said hastily, "But I don't dance."

"I know," she replied. "Just do your monkey business." She went on to explain that the menu also went wrong. They had originally ordered a smorgasbord at $2.50, but had to settle for plain swiss steak at $2.00, which meant a refund of fifty cents to each person.

In a short while I was presented. As I stepped forward to speak, I silently prayed to God for a special blessing. I didn't want to be a failure at a time like this.

As I was ending my talk, I mentioned the scholarships, needed to help Korean boys and girls who have fine minds but no funds for their education. I shall never forget a certain lady, tall and striking, who stood and asked for the floor after my talk. She moved that the refund due the members, because of the menu change, be given to the speaker for the scholarship fund. The motion was seconded and approved by a unanimous acclamation of "ayes." I received the customary honorarium plus $83.50 for scholarships.

And after all, I didn't have to dance!

CHAPTER VII

Give a man a fish, and he will eat for a day. Teach him how to fish and he will eat for the rest of his life.
—Old Oriental Proverb

My friend Eugene D. Tucci, who works at the Office of American Schools and Hospitals Abroad under the Agency for International Development, always says, "If you know how, there is no problem." The American people are especially blessed with "know-how" because they have both freedom and natural resources. Freedom can release energy, imagination, and ingenuity, but the right tools are also a necessity.

Even the brilliant sculptor Michelangelo had to have a chisel in his hand to produce unparalleled and matchless art such as his statue of *Moses*. The expression on the face of Moses is anger and pain as he watches the Hebrews dancing around the golden calf. His image looked so real that Michelangelo, striking Moses' knee with his hammer, said, "Why don't you speak?" That is the reason there is a crack on the knee of the statue of Moses.

Michelangelo said, "It is only well with me when I have a chisel in my hand." He thought of nothing but the task at hand. He ate sparingly and slept on the floor or on a cot beside his unfinished statue or painting.

But I am more interested in how you American

people have achieved a home life so comfortable and convenient by utilizing "know-how." I see the whole subject from a strictly practical point of view. In my constant travels in cities and states, I found every home, from the humblest private home to the White House, has a gas or electric range, hot and cold running water, refrigerator, washing machine, heat in the winter, air conditioning in the summer, telephones and television sets—the list seems endless. There are differences in quality, but the purpose is the same. In other countries such comforts and conveniences are limited—not common as here in the United States.

In Charles Dickens's familiar story *Oliver Twist,* one line changes the world. In a quavering voice, innocent little Oliver asks the unthinkable. He says, "Please, Sir, I want some more."

I saw the movie some years ago. Oliver Twist and the other poor children in an institution are eating a meager dish, not enough to stop their hunger, while the leaders of that institution are dining sumptuously. It was at that moment that little Oliver threw the bomb of thought. One can look back on this as one of those moments that shook the world, the point at which authority was challenged; and although it could not be known at the time, a force was set in motion which would grow and grow until it toppled institutions and introduced reforms which came to reflect a new world.

With these things in mind, I set a definite goal to help the energetic and vigorous young people of Korea learn how to make a living. I don't want just to give them fish, but to teach them how to fish, so that they can eat for the rest of their lives. For this reason, I took to the road, speaking almost constantly.

Although I have included the following story in my second book *The Hour of the Tiger,* I will have to review it here briefly because it is the crux of the whole matter, of my life. Without this experience, I could not have written this book.

There was a Korean couple in Washington, D.C., who advised me to invest my money in real estate with them. Of course I trusted them as one trusts the Bank of England. At that time the savings banks gave at best only three percent interest. Were I to invest as they suggested in real estate, I would get twice as much as the banks gave. It sounded like a wonderful opportunity to bring my Berea in Korea project closer to reality. I therefore entrusted them with the money I had earned by speaking, and continued to do so for a full six years. Practically every penny I earned in those years went into their hands. They in turn would tell me how much the profits were, and for the first few months they sent me the interest money on my original investment. After that, they "reinvested" the interest.

One day it dawned on me that for all the years my money had poured into their hands, I had no cash to show for it. So I asked them how the investment was going. The husband of this team told me that a certain amount of my money was invested in a big construction company for fifteen percent interest. My common sense told me that was too much, but my contract stated that my advisor would be responsible for the principal and interest he had invested for me.

Almost two years passed. In the meantime, my relationship with this couple became less and less friendly. I began to get suspicious that they were hiding something from me. My instincts were buzzing warnings that all was not as it should be.

Then, suddenly, my daughter and her two little boys came to America to live with me. This was an unexpected blow to that couple. They were able to fool me but not Iris. She had learned about the couple while she was still in Korea. She knew I was trapped and she wanted to save me. With much prayer, she came to America.

Less than eight months after Iris came, I was notified that my business associates had brought a lawsuit against me—charging "usury." I did not know the word and had to look it up in the dictionary. They claimed that I loaned them money at the rate of fifteen percent. Actually, it was the man who told me the money was invested in a big building construction company; it was he who typed the paper with his own fingers on his own typewriter. Now he was stabbing me in the back with a lawsuit, charging that I loaned my money to him at fifteen percent interest. When I realized what the lawsuit purported to be, I was numbed with shock. The treachery of it was absolutely appalling!

I have experienced deep tragedy. My younger daughter, Lotus, contracted tuberculosis during the long years of World War II. She had been brought back from the very edge of death by the miracle of streptomycin and months of devoted nursing, only to succumb to virus pneumonia a year and a half later. When I received word of her death, I felt as if part of my body had been severed from me—but I slept that night knowing that she rested in the Lord.

The betrayal by trusted friends brought me an agony of far different impact. Nowhere could I see the face of God. Of all the troubled nights in my life, it was the darkest and longest. The garden of Gethsemane was real to me that night!

Iris suffered as much as I did. The next morning, we looked for a lawyer to uphold my rights. I was soon to discover the reason for the suit against me was to camouflage their own wrongdoings and assure their position by threatening me.

For the next six months I maintained my busy schedule with a heavy heart. I began to realize that I was not equal to meeting such a blow spiritually. Therefore, I welcomed the opportunity to attend the Ascensiontide-Whitsuntide Retreat at Lasell House in Whitinsville, Massachusetts, under the leadership of Miss Estelle C. Carver. Where could I find a better place than the Lasell House Retreat with Miss Carver as my spiritual leader? I was in great need of a haven of rest where I could nourish both body and soul. It was definitely God's guidance.

I had been with Miss Carver several times previously at the Lasell House Retreats. She suited my temperament and understanding. She is deeply spiritual, highly intellecutal, and stands firmly on the rock. I have never met anyone who has such a brilliant mind.

Miss Carver was born in Jamaica, British West Indies, of Godly parents. Her book *Newness of Life* was dedicated to her parents who set her feet in the path of prayer and praise. In 1923 she came to New Haven, Connecticut, where she was instructor of English at Hopkins Grammar School, a college preparatory school for boys. She imparted her wealth of knowledge of the Bible, the classics, history, and literature to her pupils, and made all these subjects come alive.

Miss Carver is tall, handsome, and stately. She is in great demand as a spiritual resource leader in church groups, "Camps Farthest Out," and ashrams. She is a woman for all ages and generations. Youths are eager to hear her. Of all her followers, I am sure I have received the most.

From the beginning of the Lasell House seven-day retreat that year, I simply had no more pressing desire in life than to receive the Holy Spirit. When one receives it, one has *everything*. Miss Carver took her texts from Acts, chapter one. Every day she gave us spiritual food—twenty minutes in the forenoon, afternoon, and evening. The rest of the day each person devoted to reading, praying, and meditating.

On the third day we went into total silence for a three-and-a-half-day period—a total of eighty-four hours. There was a "balm of Gilead" all during the period of silence. During those quiet days, I often went into the small Episcopal chapel. It was peaceful and the candlelight was flickering all the time. I knelt down at the altar and poured out my heart to Christ. I made an inventory of my life in His presence. I appealed to the Lord to expose to me what was wrong in my relationship with that Korean couple. No sooner had I voiced the question when a thought flashed through my mind . . . you trusted that couple more than you trusted God. You left God completely out of the investment business from the beginning. The realization that it was true stunned me. The inner voice was right. I had trusted the couple completely, even ignoring my own conscience. What a fool I had been!

A strange thing about this situation is that, when I was in the company of my so-called friends, I had peace of mind, but the moment I left them my heart became troubled. For some reason I could not fathom, deep in my heart there was troubled water. In fact for years—ever since I sent my first check at their insistence, I had no peace of mind. Now that I look back . . . surely it was the work of the evil one.

The last night of the retreat, I went to the chapel at 11:30 p.m. and knelt at the altar with reverence, looking at the cross in the worship center. I said, "Lord, this is the last night with you in this chapel for the Ascensiontide-Whitsuntide Retreat. I am not going to leave this place unless you bless me."

Like Jacob, I wrestled with God almost half an hour. Then I relaxed and waited. Less than a few seconds later, I heard the big Westminster chime out in the hall, striking twelve times with deliberate tempo. It was midnight.

All of a sudden, a long-forgotten word came to my mind—Kyoto—Kyoto! Twenty-four years earlier, almost a quarter of a century, on November 6 at midnight I arrived in Kyoto, Japan. I was on my way to America to renew my strength after many years of marital trials and tribulations. I wanted a new deal, and my friends in

America made it possible for me to return to their wonderful country. This time, on my second trip to the States, my train stopped in Kyoto just for a couple of minutes to discharge and pick up passengers.

Kyoto at midnight! Kyoto to me was a new city, and midnight divides the old and the new day. Here I was in a new city on a new day and my new life was to be lived from that time on. Wasn't it significant that the old, forgotten city of Kyoto at midnight came to my mind? My whole being, then, became charged with new hope, power, and peace. The joy of it was unspeakable!

I could not help but say, "I have arrived." Thirty minutes before I had knelt down with a heavy heart, but now I stood up with a light heart, full of joy and comfort. That thirty minutes with Christ was like five minutes—I never even moved my fingers—I just kept one position for half an hour. I can truthfully say that I must have been transported to a seventh heaven.

I climbed the stairs and paused, looking at the Westminster chime clock with its pendulum swinging to and fro. "I became a changed, new person," I said to the clock, "while you were striking the midnight chime."

Ellen Russell, my roommate, had left our door open, knowing that I would be late coming from my prayers. So I tiptoed in and hopped into bed, for I was dressed to retire before going to the chapel. It was a dark night, without a moon, but the stars were twinkling brightly. I could see them from my bed. What a different night it was compared with the night when the lawsuit was brought against me six months before. That had been full of anxiety, worry, heartache, but now there was joy, forgiveness, and compassion. I went to sleep full of thanksgiving and praise.

In the midst of my deep sleep I was awakened by a heavy, ugly, harsh voice saying, "It cannot be done!"

I said, "What?"

The voice answered, "The lawsuit cannot be won.

Berea in Korea will never be realized."

By this time my heart was beating so fast and throbbing so loudly I almost felt suffocated. Then the sensation of sinking overtook me—sinking down, down. I pressed my hand over my heart, and in an inaudible voice I said, "God, it can be done!"

Then a light! It was a rich, deep blue, laced with royal purple—such as I had never seen in my whole life. It was rectangular in shape and full of floating geometrical figures, triangles, squares, and ovals. The size appeared to be about a foot and a half by eight inches. The entire picture was pulsating—increasing and decreasing in a rhythmic manner. While it was repeated three times, I watched with wonder and awe, lying in bed.

When the light disappeared, I said, "God, you have given me tangible assurance with light and color that my prayer has been heard."

The next morning when I arose I found a new world full of his glory. I never before saw New England in May so fresh and beautiful. Every tree was budding out, so dainty and green. It was a glorious May 16 for me. I was fairly bursting with a long-forgotten song:

> I sing because I'm happy,
> I sing because I'm free.
> For His eye is on the sparrow
> And I know He watches me.

No wonder the one hundred twenty in the Upper Room were charged—being "filled with new wine," after they received the Holy Spirit. I realized I was definitely charged and changed—the old self for the new. Even the world was unfolding its new spring wardrobe. How refreshing! How exciting! How thrilling!

After the Lasell House experience I looked back on the previous horrible, tempestuous six months and, even though they were the worst ones in my life, they all dissolved away like a heap of suds. Now the whole world seemed quiet and peaceful; absolute tranquility reigned in my heart. I felt as though I were once more anchored in God—looking out at the troubled sea where the masses of people were tossing and striving.

Since my spiritual renewal, my entire attitude and emphasis have changed. Before, I thought I had to make money for Berea in Korea. I, I, I . . . always I felt I had a good reason for doing this. God had no hands and feet but mine. So I had to do it for him. But now I follow his command . . . "Seek first his kingdom and his righteousness and all these things shall be yours" (Matthew 6:33, RSV). Now for me it is "To live is Christ." Oh! I was beaten mercilessly by the forces of evil because of my shortcomings. Since that time, I literally live by this verse: "I am the vine, you are the branches. He who abides in me and I in him, he it is that bears much fruit, for apart from me you can do nothing" (John 15:5). Like a fish in water, I must abide in him; otherwise, I will die.

After my spiritual rebirth, wherever I went to speak, both the audience and myself were electrified, charged. The comments made by the audience were very different before and after my new spiritual experience. *Before*, people said, "How interesting your speech was! How eloquently you speak! You show your country and her needs very well."

But *after*, people said, "You are a little bundle of dynamite! Your power is being generated by your faith and prayer. What can we do for you and your people?"

The next two years I made at least as much, if not more, money than what I had lost in ten years. How? Before, when an invitation came for a speaking engagement and the amount of the honorarium was requested, I would write and designate the amount. Of course, I was given that amount exactly. But after, I left the entire matter to God and in the hands of the inviting party, saying that I was working for Berea in Korea, a pilot project. As a result, the amounts given doubled and tripled—beyond my fondest expectation. Once I was after money. Now money is after me. I let God open the money reservoir and out it pours through audiences and friends. And so for the next two years everything was tops! God gave me enough funds to go to Korea and actually start the Berea in Korea project.

What happened to the lawsuit? After my Lasell House experience, I thought of the whole case from my associates' point of view. I could forgive them as God had forgiven me. So I signed off and the case was closed. To this day, I do not know where they live. It seems no Korean knows their whereabouts. If I ever see them again, I want to thank them for what they did to me. Had they not brought the lawsuit, I would never have had such a glorious spiritual experience.

I am reminded of the following story. When St. Paul went to heaven, he encountered St. Stephen to whom he said, "St. Stephen, I could never forgive myself for what I did to you." St. Stephen replied, "Had you not done that to me, you would never have become St. Paul."

I lost my money, but I found God.

Exactly two years after my marvelous spiritual experience, May 15, 1961, I left for Korea to start my Berea in Korea project. News of a revolution's starting in Korea came twelve hours before my departure from Washington, D.C. All my friends including Iris advised me not to proceed, but I knew what I was doing. God was in this plan.

That year, Mrs. Easter Lily Gates and Mrs. T. L. Marquis went to the Orient with me. By the time we arrived in Seoul on June 29, after visiting nine other Eastern countries, the Korean government had changed hands peacefully, from Dr. Chang to General Park Chung Hee.

After my friends returned to the United States, I spent the rest of the summer searching for the most suitable location for our school. Just five days before my departure for America, I found a thirty-acre tract of land in Seoul, seven miles from the heart of the city. A big mountain stands back of it and a river flows next to it, but there were no roads leading directly to it, no water, no light, but many, many old graves. From the ordinary Korean point of view, it appeared to be more of a liability than an asset. But at first sight, I saw in my mind's eye Berea in Korea rising on this spot.

I am reminded of a girl who saw a large piece of marble in the studio of her employer, a sculptor. Some months later, the marble had been transformed into the bust of a famous man. The girl remarked, "I didn't know there was a bust of a man in that piece of marble.

In spite of the consensus of my friends and acquaintances, who considered my choice of property totally unwise, I made up my mind to purchase that land. I knew what I was doing because God was doing it through me. I had perfect peace of mind and went through the legal procedures. The rain was torrential all this time as we discussed the price. But after the seller and I agreed to the price and signed the paper, the rain stopped and the afternoon sun shone brightly in the blue sky, playing hide and seek with the white clouds.

Now I had the land for Berea in Korea. That was half the battle.

On Easter Sunday, a year and seven months after the purchase of the land, we broke ground for the first building. It was the most solemn moment of my life. My reason for choosing Easter Sunday for the occasion was to commemorate the coming of the first Methodist missionaries, Dr. and Mrs. Henry G. Appenzeller of Lancaster, Pennsylvania, to Korea. Had they and Mrs. Mary Scranton not come and founded Ewha, Berea in Korea would never have been.

Then preparation for construction started. First of all, the old graves had to be removed. There were more than two hundred old graves, I was told. With the government's consent, we put an ad in the paper for weeks. When no one turned up to claim any of the graves, a group of men took charge of the task and cleared the property. The occupants of the graves did not object! All went to another public cemetery.

By this arrangement, I inherited seventy-six magnificent granite tombstones and tables. With some we constructed a tombstone gate for the school, which we call "Resurrection Gate." I believe it is unique. Others were used for stone flooring in the entrance to the main building.

After the old graves were removed, we started searching for a source of water. No one had built in this valley previously because there was no water. It had been known as a dry valley for ages. There was some surface water during the rainy season, but it was completely arid the rest of the year. The whole area has rocks, rocks, and more rocks, all over. When I bought this property, I did not know of the existance of such a crucial problem—no water. Had I known it, I would not have purchased the land.

But I was sure there had to be water somewhere in this property, or God would not have led me to it. With Iris's cousin Nam-Kyu Chung, who was helping me, I started exploring. When I came to a certain spot, I stopped suddenly. I felt I could hear water running under my feet. So I turned to Nam-Kyu and said, "Bring me four men tomorrow and let them dig here until they get water."

He was almost shocked to hear me saying this so positively. He said, "Auntie, there is no water in this valley. I will do as you say, but don't expect any water. You will just waste your money."

I said, "Do as I tell you."

The next day the men came and dug for a week.

They went down sixteen feet and then the rock!

I thought to myself, Moses met the Red Sea but I, rock! Instantly I said, "God, what am I going to do next?" A wonderful thought was given to me from the story of how Moses got water by striking the rock with his rod. Why not strike the rock? With what? There were many, many centuries between Moses' time and mine. He struck the rock with his rod and got water, but I would strike my rock with dynamite!

Two men who knew how to use dynamite were brought in the next day. They looked into the deep hole and said, "We may dynamite all the way to Washington, D.C., but there won't be any water."

I replied, "Then make a tunnel and we will get water from the Potomac River."

In two hours the rock was dynamited, and through the cracked rocks water was gushing out! I screamed, "This water is coming from the Potomac River!" Later we had the water tested—it is about one hundred percent pure.

While going through this exciting experience, I couldn't help but think that one's life leaps like a geyser when he drills through the rock of inertia.

My next problem was to move a hill. When I saw it, it was just a hill, but when I had to move it, it looked like a mountain. I said to Nam-Kyu, "You see the hill? That has to go. It's in my way."

He replied, "That hill will never go away."

The answer came from your American "know-how." God may not need my intelligence, but he certainly cannot use my ignorance. "Education may be expensive, but ignorance is even more costly," someone said.

I said, "Bring me a bulldozer with three men."

He did, and it took exactly one hundred eight hours to move that hill.

The whole hill filled up the ravine and made it into an athletic field for our school. Every time I see the athletic field where our boys play, I think of the hill that stood there for ages. Now it is comfortably lying down in the valley, resting forever. At the same time, it serves as an athletic field, helping our boys become strong and vigorous, physically and mentally, for ages to come.

Finally, we erected two buildings, one for the classrooms and offices, the other for the dormitory and dining room. The construction funds were provided largely by my long-standing friend, Mrs. Katherine S. Armington of Ohio, and the Kresge Foundation of Michigan. We set the cornerstone for the main building, Armington-Kresge Hall, on the Fourth of July to commemorate the Independence Day of the United States of America, and dedicated both buildings, still unfinished, on September 24, 1963. Joining the celebration were eleven friends who had accompanied me on my first Orient Tour: two from Canada—Ethel M. Dean and Doris W. Courtice; and nine from the United States— Katherine S. Armington, Ruth Ferguson, Betty Hubbard, Elva E. Martin, Margaret K. Patterson, Mildred Pope, Marie and Merwyn Skidmore, and Florence Stevens.

After the construction was finished, we advertised the opening of a work-study high school and got one hundred fifty applications. Of that number, we selected thirty whom we thought were physically fit and mentally alert. At last, on March 20, 1964, I actually opened Berea in Korea with thirty boys in the tenth grade, and seven staff members. It was the day a little acorn was planted.

Why a boys' school? I will reserve the reason for the next chapter in this book. That opening day was the crowning moment of my life, for I had worked and prayed for thirty-five long years. On that day I found my pearl of great price, Berea in Korea (Induk Vocational High School). Our young people will learn how to fish so that they can eat for the rest of their lives.

It is almost too good to be true! Praise God!

CHAPTER VIII

He who sows sparingly will also reap sparingly, and
he who sows bountifully will also reap bountifully.
—2 Corinthians 9:6, RSV

In the last page of my second book, *The Hour of the
Tiger*, I said how much I would love to stay at my new
school and watch it grow, but I had to return to
America to tell my friends about it instead. I said, "My
daughter Iris Kim will be here on the scene with her
most productive years still ahead of her, running the
school, keeping my dream alive."

My prediction was right. A year after our school was
founded, Iris spent six months in Korea sizing up the
situation. She returned to America and told me she
would take over the school. It was God's provenance.
She had learned how to conduct an orchestra with a little baton; now the school is her orchestra.

Iris did not just jump into this responsibility without
thinking. She prayed about it and made her decision in
His presence. When she needs wisdom, she knows the
source: the Bible. "If any of you lack wisdom, he should
pray to God, who will give it to him, for God gives
generously and graciously." Indeed, she is well-fortified.

With this in mind, she found two of my close
friends, who gave her valuable suggestions in running
the school. One was Chae-Hoh Lee, a brilliant patent

lawyer who gave Iris some wonderful ideas. The other was Dr. Pong-Cho Shin who was principal of Ewha Girls' High School (Iris's alma mater, and mine) for twenty-five years. He taught her from an administrator's point of view. Both men live in Seoul and give their advice freely. What wonderful friends they have been to Iris all these years!

Even with this fine counsel, Iris's orchestra would not play well; sometimes it was too slow, or too fast, or out of tune, or jarred. But she kept on with one hundred boys in the dormitory and eighteen on the staff. In the early years, all the boys lived in the dormitory with two cooks and a housemother. Every time Iris had trouble, she would read the Bible, pray, and seek out one of her two friends.

In her second year, which was the third year after the founding of our school, the Double Dragon Cement Company bought up the land next to our campus, with plans to build a factory. First, they started building a road to transport building material. This was all done without consulting Iris. In the midst of building the road, the president of the company, whose son I had brought to America to be educated, called Iris into his office and said, "We are going to build a cement factory next to your school. In fact, we have already begun. I want you to sell your school to us and move out of the city where the land is cheaper. You can buy a piece of property much bigger than this to build your school. I am doing you a favor."

Iris looked straight at him with all her dignity and might, and replied, "Why don't *you* move out? It would be much cheaper for you because we have already built our school and you are just beginning. Furthermore, yours is a factory; ours is a school where we train boys to run factories.

"You recall that my mother stayed at your home in the summer of 1961 and that your wife helped her look around Seoul to find a tract of land on which to build a school. She spotted this site and signed the deed in your house on September 1, 1961," Iris continued. "I want you to answer my question with one word—yes or no. Are you willing to give up your life for your cement factory? My mother and I are willing to give up our lives for our school."

It was Iris's first grave trial. She contacted some influential men and women for assistance in this trying case, but many were helpless because the Double Dragon Cement Company had money and powerful political backing. No one dared to touch it. It would be like touching a beehive.

But Iris had the most powerful backing of all—God Almighty of justice and righteousness. She was given wisdom and courage to present her case to Madam Park, wife of President Park Chung Hee, through a friend of hers. Madam Park investigated the case through the "Public Grievance Department" and stopped the Double Dragon Cement Company from building its factory next to our school. We won this case by the interaction of God through Madame Park. Do you wonder why Iris and I depend upon God totally and absolutely?

When I heard of this predicament from Iris, I prayed that God would show the Double Dragon Cement Company a far better location for their factory. We have a saying that you must provide leeway for your enemy to escape. Indeed, God answered my prayers. While the case was in the hands of the Public Grievance Committee, the cement company found a location much more suitable than the one next to our campus; it is just ten miles away—but far better for both of us.

Who could take away our school property? No one. God put aside this particular place thousands of years ago for us to honor and glorify him. We will prove ourselves worthy of it. The following pages will tell how we have made use of that God-given location.

Berea in Korea (Induk Vocational High School for boys) is designed to: 1) train boys to live a well-rounded, useful life, beginning in the dormitory (we take 120 first-year boys for six weeks at a time), practicing "God first, others second, myself last"; and, 2) teach boys to create something out of nothing, using their hands and heads. The whole school revolves around these two precepts.

In order to fulfill the purpose of our school, we worked out a curriculum which will help our boys discover their hidden talents and develop their skills.

We teach arts and sciences in addition to such practical subjects as gardening and landscaping, animal husbandry, and carpentry. Lately, we have added mechanical engineering, civil engineering, metallurgy, architecture, ceramics, and arts and crafts.

Why a boys' school? Knowing of my difficulties as a girl in getting an education, many people ask me this question. There are very important reasons behind my decision to teach boys.

Korea now has schools for girls, both public and private. Some are vocational schools where girls may learn teaching, nursing, medicine, law, and secretarial work as well as hairdressing, homemaking, cooking, and sewing. Furthermore, all the men's universities are now coeducational.

There are vocational high schools for boys besides ours. But the emphasis we have in our school is to use hands not to make things only, but *to serve*. We want our boys to dedicate their hands to their families, communities, and country. This spirit in action will be of untold help to their mothers and wives. Up to now, cooking, sewing, washing, cleaning—all the manual work around the home—was left to mothers, sisters, and wives. Then men take it for granted and never think how difficult it is.

We want to help our boys break away from this old

traditional habit of thinking and form new attitudes toward the duties and responsibilities of men. We teach our boys to clean their own rooms and classrooms, to set and wait on tables, and even to wash dishes. I don't believe there is any other school such as ours anywhere in Korea.

Man wants to be waited on according to the age-old custom, not only in my country but in other countries, too—even in the days of Jesus, this was so. I read in the Bible about Jesus' visit to the home of Mary, Martha, and Lazarus in Bethany. A banquet was prepared in Jesus' honor. It is written that Martha served and Lazarus sat at the table.

Our boys disliked washing dishes and sweeping yards; but in our school they had to, whether they liked it or not, because it was part of the curriculum. When the first weekend came to go home after a month's discipline in working and studying, we told them not to let their grandmothers, mothers, or sisters sweep the yard in the morning. That was the first thing each should remember.

Second, when they boarded a streetcar or bus, they should let the elders, women, and girls get on first. Third, if they saw a woman carrying a bundle on her head and a baby on her back, they should offer to carry the bundle.

The boys returned to school after the weekend at home. The first thing I asked was whether they remembered what they were asked to do. Quite a few of them raised their hands. I asked them how they felt. One boy said modestly, "I got up ahead of my family and swept the yard as I do at school. I felt happy because I did my duty as a man."

Then I asked how many of them let women and girls get on the bus first. Only one boy raised his hand, and said, "By the time I let them on first, there was no room for me and the bus pulled out. I had to wait twenty-five minutes for the next bus!"

A week later, the grandmother of one of the boys came to our school and asked to see me. I thought there must be some problem. No parents had come to the school previously unless there was a problem. The elderly grandmother was led to my office. Just to look at her face, I knew instinctively she must have something special to tell me.

When she said, "What did you do to my grandson?" I did not say anything, just listened. She continued, "He got up early and swept the yard for the first time in his life. After breakfast, he even offered to wash the dishes!"

She asked her grandson why he did those things which he had never done before.

He answered, "Grandma, it's a boy's job, not yours."

I asked her, "Did you like it?"

"Did I like it! I loved it! I am glad your school teaches my grandson and other boys how to help their mothers and sisters at home."

I felt I was justified in founding a boys' school.

The other most important reason for founding a boys' school is to help erase the gap between scholars and peasants. For centuries, Korea had developed only the heads of the scholars and the hands of the peasants, creating a deep chasm between them.

For the last 500 years of the Yi Dynasty, the government was in the hands of scholars who studied Chinese classics and passed the royal examinations. Every young man had but one ambition in those days— to pass the royal examination so that he could qualify to become a prime minister or other high official in the government. Should he achieve this, he suddenly had thrust upon him glory, honor, and wealth. The whole nation was in the palm of his hand. But although many tried, few achieved their goal.

Those few ruled the country—not understanding

the life of the majority of the people who toiled from dawn to dusk, using their hands. There was such a deep, wide gap between mental and manual labor that there was no communication. Through our school for boys, daringly we attempt to eliminate that gap. "Attempt great things for God, and expect great things from him." We rolled up our sleeves and started working toward our goal—the dignity of labor.

I am simply amazed how our students and teachers exercise our school motto: "With hand and head create something out of nothing." In our ceramics class, I watch our boys express their hopes and feelings using a lump of insensate clay. Each boy creates something beautiful and useful. When I watch, I cannot help but think how much Korea has lost by not realizing the value of using hands.

Some seven or eight hundred years ago Korea produced famous porcelain, but the skill has been lost as the generations changed. I may be wrong, but I think the disdain for using hands might have been the cause of it. Men set their minds and thoughts only to scholarship. Thoughts are powerful, but we cannot eat thoughts. They must be realized; this involves hands.

Korea has also been known for particularly fine-beaten brassware. It is now one of the lost arts because of the handwork required. Modern metallurgy has never been able to duplicate the process or imitate the luster of the ware. The process by which the bowls were made was primitive but meticulously supervised. The copper ore, containing small quantities of silver, was mined at Kapsan near the Yalu River. Tin ingots were brought from China to Ansung, about sixty miles south of Seoul, where the smelting was done by skilled craftsmen.

Many of the secrets of this ancient art have been lost, but this much is known: the rough ore was first melted into a solid ingot over a pinewood charcoal fire which contained no sulphuric acid gas and maintained an even temperature. The solid ingot was then returned to the fire and heated to a fixed temperature; this was one of the critical points in the process.

When it reached exactly the right temperature, the ingot was beaten into roughly the shape desired. Then it was curved by a unique method requiring repeated submerging in water, until the bowl took the desired shape.

Because of the long and tedious process required to make these bowls, they were very expensive and only royalty, nobility, and the very wealthy could afford to use the ware. Today, this antique hammered brassware is highly prized and considered to be superior to brass produced in China, Japan, or India.

How can one recognize genuine hammered brassware? It has an exceptionally smooth polish, a beautiful luster, and a color resembling old eighteen-karat yellow gold. Most significant, it has a beautiful, bell-like tone when struck—deep and resonant. My mother gave me a water bowl of hammered brass which I treasure. Every time I polish it, I think of the craftsmen who produced such unexcelled pieces of brassware long ago with hands and head.

Since I recognize the beauty of ancient Korean porcelain and hammered brassware, I want all the more to provide opportunities to Korean youth for learning skills, today. My enthusiasm is accentuated by thoughts of Jesus' working in a carpentry shop making yokes and plows. I am sure his hands were hardened from toil. A man who works with his hands is a laborer, but a man who works with his hands and his brain is a craftsman. We read in the Old Testament that craftsmanship is the gift of the spirit of God.

The Lord said to Moses, "See, I have appointed Bezalel . . . and have filled him with the spirit of God, giving him great wisdom, ability, and skill in constructing the tabernacle and everything it contains. He is highly capable as an artistic designer of objects made of gold, silver, and bronze. He is skilled, too, as a jeweler and in carving wood" (Exodus 31:1–5, *The Living Bible*).

While reading the above verses in the Bible, I could hear the crash of the hammer, the buzz of the saw, and the noise of the chisel on the stone, breaking the silence into an active life. Korea has been too quiet for too long a time; but, through modern education in technology, we can see the old Korean mind being awakened by the rhythmic noise of working with hands and heads.

The mission of our school in this transition is to put the spirit of God into it—to make a pleasing rhythm of noise instead of *just noise*.

Under the leadership of my daughter Iris Kim, our school has grown by leaps and bounds. Iris lives in the domitory with the boys. The dormitory can accommodate 120 boys at a time. Each boy spends six weeks of his first year living in the dormitory where he receives spiritual training. They get other training in their classes from the teachers, but Iris emphasizes the spiritual side of life.

In each room there are two tiers of bunk beds, so four boys live together. Sleeping in a bed is a new experience for most of the boys. At home, they sleep on the floor in an *ondol* room; Korean homes have a unique heating system called *ondol*. Under the floor are a number of flues covered with flat stones. The floor is papered with extra-thick oiled paper coated with varnish. To protect the surface, we remove our shoes when we enter a room.

The flues are, of course, connected to the chimney. The fire is built in the kitchen. We usually have three built-in cooking kettles set in a row, first a large one, a smaller size next, and a third still smaller. There is an opening where we build the fire, using wood, coal, or briquettes. When we cook, we boil water in the big kettle, rice in the middle-sized one, and soup in the smallest. The cook knows how to regulate the temperature of the fire, how much is needed for boiling water, cooking rice, etc. While cooking, the smoke and heat go through the flues and heat the rooms.

In summer, we cook outdoors and only air circulates through the flues. In this way, we have built-in air conditioners, too. They are not completely satisfactory, but better than nothing.

As I said, sleeping in a bed is a new experience for our boys. The housemother teaches them how to make the bed. When one goes through our domitory, the rooms look almost like a military school. We teach the boys cleanliness and orderliness.

During the spring, summer (we have a month's vacation in the summer), and fall, the boys are awakened at 5:45 in the morning by a chime. It starts softly and gets louder and louder. I have been with them in the morning, and the chime sounds as though it is ringing from heaven when all is quiet at dawn.

The early morning chime at our school reminds me of a Buddhist monk in a temple beating a wooden bell at three in the morning while he is praying. I have heard it myself. Every morning the monk was the first to break the absolute silence of the mountainside where the Buddhist temple stood.

But in our school, we announce the new day with a chime. For hundreds of years, our valley had no such chime.

The chimes arouse the school. In five minutes the boys dress and rush out to the athletic field to jog for five minutes. By this time they are wide awake. They go through a gymnastic exercise to music, recite the school motto, and rush to the dining room where Iris waits for them. They tiptoe into the room with absolute quietness while Iris greets them with a smile. She chooses a hymn for the day and plays the reed organ while the boys sing. Morning devotions take half an hour.

Only one-fourth of the first-year boys come from Christian homes, but the non-Christian boys also learn to sing, read the Bible, and pray while they live in the dormitory. Every morning Iris teaches them how to sing, how to read the Bible, and how to pray. This is her particular mission in school. In six weeks they memorize the Lord's Prayer, the Ten Commandments, the First and the Twenty-third Psalms, and other scriptures.

Iris does not beg them to be Christians, but she makes it so exciting that they feel they are left out if they don't get into the fold. They beg to learn more about it. Iris tells me there is such a difference in the thinking and attitude of the boys before and after they enter the dormitory. It is like heaven and earth.

After devotions, the boys clean their rooms, classrooms, halls, and walks, spick-and-span. We are generous with trash cans and the boys learn to use them.

Breakfast is at 7:30. When the bell rings, all go to the dining room. Each takes a tray of food from the kitchen. On the tray, one will find a bowl of rice, soup, and a dish of *kimchi,* with a pair of chopsticks and a spoon.

Koreans are known for *kimchi.* We cut cabbage, turnips, and celery; add salt, hot pepper, onions, garlic, ginger, and nuts; then mix it all together and put it in an earthen jar to ferment. We have so many different variations—for winter, summer, spring, and fall, that we have more than Heinz's fifty-seven varities. *Kimchi* is a perfect balance to our rice diet which we eat three times a day, all year around.

Before starting to eat, the boys sing a song thanking God for food and asking him to bless all those who made it possible for them to eat. We always post a Bible verse in the dining room for the boys to read. It is carefully designed and written to attract their attention.

Singing plays a very important part in our school. We sing because we are grateful for life, hope, and opportunities. We also know the power of song. Miracles take place when people sing.

Consider a story from the Old Testament (2 Chronicles 20). When the kings of Moab, Ammon, and the Meunites declared war on Judah, King Jehoshaphat immediately called his people to pray to God, with penitence and fasting. While they were praying, a message came to one of them from God saying that the battle was not theirs but God's. They were so grateful that they worshipped God with songs of praise. The people were told that they need not fight but go down, stand quietly, and watch the incredible rescue operation God would perform for them.

Early the next morning, the army of Judah went out into the wilderness of Tekoa. While they were there, King Jehoshaphat and his advisors decided to let a choirmaster lead the march from then on; they were clothed in sanctified garments and singing the song "His Loving-kindness Is Forever," as they walked along praising and thanking the Lord.

At the moment they began to sing and praise him, the Lord caused their enemies to begin fighting among themselves, and they destroyed each other! So the army of Judah, led by a choir, did not have to fight. From a distance, they just watched their enemies fighting and destroying each other.

Now you know why our boys sing. Our school is just thirty-five miles south of Panmunjom. Like the people of Judah challenged by their enemies, we are challenged by North Korean Communists. This is a reality. We will have to face it and win in the end without actual fighting. How?

First, we sing to North Korea every day in our school. As we sing, we send our love and concern for our brothers and sisters over there. We are positive that the vibration of our singing carries our message to them!

106

Second, we have worn the armor of God: truth, righteousness, peace, and faith. We are ever ready to meet the evil forces anytime, anywhere. We are ever alert and never give up because God is our supreme Commander-in-Chief.

Besides spiritual armament, we give our boys a thorough military training, as do all the other boys' schools. We teach them karate, too, but it is optional; the purpose is for self-protection. To have it and not need it is better than to need it and not have it.

Iris is dedicated and devoted to the school, next to her God and her two sons, but she is lavish and extravagant with her love for what she is doing. Starting with herself, Iris wants every teacher and every staff member to know what each is doing and to love and appreciate what each one knows.

Iris has a favorite story she tells the beginning class each year: "One day a minister in a small town drove up to a poor family's house. The little children rushed out of the house and saw his shiny, black Buick, and admired it greatly. The minister said, 'This car was given to me by my brother.' One little boy said, 'Gee, I wish I could have a brother like that', as he touched the car. But an older boy said in a serious and thoughtful tone, 'Oh! How I wish I could be like that brother!' "

Iris tries to develop "brothers." Just over the hill from our school, there is a village called Kok-Sim-Jul with forty-five families. This is one of the poor villages bordering Seoul. The villagers make a living by farming, growing rice, wheat, and vegetables. Soon after we brought electricity to our school, we told the village elder that we would be glad to give his village electricity from ours. But he turned us down, saying that kerosene is cheaper and they had been using it for all these years.

Then the village people passed by our school and saw the bright electric lights. They asked us to give electricity to their village. Gladly, our teachers and students went to Kok-Sim-Jul and helped them put up and wire the poles. When the light was turned on, the old, poor, dark village became a modern village of light. What a thrill it was! "Let there be light, and there was light."

Our next project was to put in a sewer in Kok-Sim-Jul. Our civil engineering class helped the village men dig ditches and put in earthen pipes so that the water wouldn't run all over the village. Sanitation at home and in the community is of great concern in teaching our students.

Some years later, when I was at our school, the village elder of Kok-Sim-Jul called on me and said, "Your school gave us light and sewer. We cannot live without you!" What a gratifying statement that was!

In the ten years of Iris's tenure, she has produced 360 graduates from our Induk Vocational High School. More than one-half of the graduates are employed in various fields; our graduates have no problem finding jobs because we trained them to meet the public's needs. Seven came to America as immigrants with their families; thirty-two entered higher institutes, five of whom entered our own Induk Institute of Design. Ninety-nine, more than one-fourth of the graduates, have started their own projects. Every graduate has found his place in life. I want to tell you, more specifically, what a few have done since graduation.

Case No. 1. In-Kyo Kim is one of the first graduates of our school. Being an only son, he was exempted from army service. His father died soon after he was born, and his mother became a seamstress. In-Kyo saw the ad we put in the paper announcing our new Vocational High School. He came to school with his mother and grandmother. They told me of their hardships in educating him.

He was not a brilliant student, but he was an honest and hard-working boy. He graduated in February, 1967, with seventeen others in the first graduating class of our school. Upon his graduation, he leased a small half-acre plot near the village of Ahnyang and started a rose-culture farm. The following year, he leased almost an acre of land near Seoul. He hoped to make it a city of roses. I went to his rose-culture farm soon after he moved in. He had put up a tent and his mother and grandmother were living with him, helping with the garden.

In-Kyo needed capital. He asked Iris for a loan, and she helped him for several years. Today, he has paid back to the school every penny he owed. He employs several men and women during the height of the season and clears a good profit. I hear he is experimenting with new colors of roses.

Case No. 2. Jang-Sub Pahk graduated in the fourth class. He returned to his village in Kyunggi Province and cleared a hillside all by himself, about an acre. It took him a long time, but he finally succeeded. He planted soybeans, which do not require fertilizer, along with other vegetables. With his profit he purchased a heifer. Now he owns seven cows, and he and his family are making a good living on the farm. During the long winter months, he gives lectures on how to make a living using hands and head to young men from his own and nearby villages. Instead of cursing the darkness, he lit a candle which shines brightly in his own community.

Case No. 3. Three of our graduates heard of Jang-Sub's pioneer work and have started clearing a hillside of about seventeen acres, quite an ambitious undertaking. But they will make it, I am sure. I am eager to know how they will use the land, for it is located in an historically important area. Whatever they do, they will make it most productive land.

Case No. 4. San-Dong Kim, a graduate of the seventh class, started a poultry-breeding business. He made his own incubator apparatus and produces 150,000 baby chicks every year. Won-Myung Pahk is another graduate who started a poultry farm.

Case No. 5. Jung-Soo Kim was given a pair of young pigs by his junior high school alma mater. He started a pig farm with them and has increased his stock to ten pairs. He loves his pigs so much that he knows the temperament, likes, and dislikes of each pig. How lucky Jung-Soo's pigs are!

Case No. 6. Eight graduates united and started a New Village Movement in Yichun County, Kyunggi Province, under the motto "With God All Things Are Possible." They have made this movement attractive and exciting to the young people of that county, even publishing a small paper called *Good Earth.* Together, they clear useless lands, plant fruit trees, and grow vegetables. In the evenings they gather together eighty children and teach them how to sing and play cooperatively.

I want to make special note of our teachers, also. Again, not all are Christians. We do not ask them to embrace our religion, just make it worthwhile for them to try. Our dean, Jin-Chul Kim, is a perfect example. He was not a Christian but Iris took him to church every Sunday. Gradually he learned, was baptized, and joined the church. He had not known how to sing, but I heard him singing, reading his Bible, and praying. It was a miracle!

It is very gratifying to see the faculty in our school getting better, happier, and richer spiritually and economically. They have moved into better homes since they came to us—one has even built a new home. They like to live near the school.

We have six major buildings on our campus now, all brick, and eleven smaller cement buildings. Iris never uses a general contract company in construction. Since the beginning, our school has been its own contractor. The school has purchased or manufactured the necessary building materials and hired the required labor directly. To date our school has achieved great success in construction.

110

In the years since Induk Vocational High School was established, Seoul has grown by leaps and bounds, and the area between downtown Seoul and our school is much built up. The population of Seoul reached seven million in the fall of 1975.

Korea's need for the type of education our school provides is very great. Therefore, we must achieve maximum benefit for each dollar spent; Iris tries to stretch every dollar given by our friends to its limit!

CHAPTER IX

I am the Lord, the God of all mankind; is there
anything too hard for me?

—Jeremiah 32:37

"How are you, Sister Induk?" I looked up. Standing before me was E. Stanley Jones, founder of Christian Ashrams. I hadn't seen him for several years, yet he could
call my name with no hesitation. What a marvelous
memory he has! It is one secret of his charisma.

I was attending the Keuka Ashram in 1971, and it
was now the last day. There are two very important ses-
sions at an Ashram. The first is an "open heart" session
at the beginning. Each participant tells his name and
address, church affiliation, and business. After this meeting we all become brothers and sisters in Christ.

The other session takes place on closing day. It is
called "overflow," perhaps because our hearts overflow
as each one tells what he got out of the Ashram. There
is quite a difference even in one's appearance between
"open heart" and "overflow." There is a jubilance
among the people. In a week, one's attitudes and thinking are changed from negative to positive, discourage-
ment to encouragement, and dull life to hope and excitement.

At the Keuka Ashram I had one particular prayer
project—to build a new classroom building for our voca-

tional high school. With our increasing school population, we had to provide more space. It would cost quite a sum of money, and we had only enough to build the foundation with the money given by the Kresge Foundation. When Iris told me how much it would cost, I said, "Just build the first two stories." Even at that, I didn't have the funds, but I knew they would come.

For six months I had been praying, but nothing happened until I got to the Keuka Ashram in July. At the "overflow" session on Friday morning, July 23, 1971, at 11:00, as I was getting up to tell what had happened to me during the Ashram, a sentence flashed through my mind, "I am the Lord, the God of all mankind; is there anything too hard for me?"

I answered, "No, Lord. With you all things are possible."

Truthfully, I did not know then that this verse was Jeremiah 32:27. I felt awed! I did not have the slightest idea where the needed funds for the building would come from, but I knew they would come in God's good time. I did not have them in my hand, but I felt exactly as if I did.

Upon my return from the Keuka Ashram, I found a letter awaiting my arrival. It was from Mrs. Harlow M. Russell of Boothbay Harbor, Maine. In it she wrote, "My husband and I have discussed your school in Korea. With much prayer and thought, we have decided to give you our summer cottage, 'Morning Glory,' to build a vocational high school building. We do not know how much it will bring, but we will deed it to your foundation. Since you are leaving with your Orient tour in less than two weeks, we will arrange the legal details so that you will have it when you return to America in September."

I held the letter in my hand and repeated what God said to me at Keuka, "Is there anything too hard for me?" This letter was entirely unexpected. But when the

113

Lord speaks, he starts working. He works on both ends, the giver and the receiver.

The Russells live in St. Petersburg, Florida, during the winter months. When Mrs. Russell read in the St. Petersburg paper in January, 1971, that a Korean was to speak, she wanted to see me because she was helping an orphanage in Pusan. We met at Ruth Cotton's home. Mrs. Russell had been very much interested in the orphanage for some years and donated generously to it. I have a special feeling for those who help Korea, especially with orphans. Therefore, from the beginning I considered her as a special friend, not only to me but to Korea as a whole.

I was much interested in her husband's work, also. He started working with his father when he graduated from high school and directed the Russell Box Company until 1943. Over the years his firm produced billions of different kinds of boxes, for coughdrops, gum, ice cream, paper clips—almost anything. He remembered that Ludens once ordered five billion boxes for their coughdrops.

Among the innovations Mr. Russell developed was the paper packages for salt and pepper now used by many airlines. He was on a United Airlines flight to Pittsburgh when he showed his new salt container to a stewardess. She, in turn, showed it to airline officials. In two weeks he had a wire: "How much, and how soon can we have them?"

Mr. Russell told me the idea for those salt and pepper containers came from corrugated paper. Every time I see them, I think of the Russell Box Company.

Since he retired, Mr. Russell is devoted to religious communication. He has been recording sermons at Pasadena Community Church in St. Petersburg since 1948 and sending them to his friends in the Northeast. In 1958, after visiting the Protestant Radio and Television Center in Atlanta, he began supplying taped sermons to libraries and theological seminaries throughout the United States. Thus far, tapes have been sent to 105 seminaries across America and in other countries.

Mr. Russell celebrated his ninety-ninth birthday in 1975, but he still works daily making recordings. He goes to church every Sunday no matter what the weather and records the sermon. He is one of the greatest philanthropists I have ever met.

When I returned from my third Orient tour in September, 1971, a letter enclosing a deed for the Russells' summer cottage "Morning Glory," legally transferred to our foundation, was waiting for my arrival. What a welcome God gave me through the Russells! They even found a buyer for the cottage.

"It was a miracle," Ruth Russell said in her letter. The minute they decided to give the house to our foundation, a man called, wanting to buy the property. A check for $35,707.28 came to our foundation.

"Is there anything too hard for me?"

"No, Lord."

Soon after I returned from Korea that year, I got an invitation from Lucile Sewell in Annapolis, Maryland, to spend a few days with her and her husband William. I met sister Lucile at the Keuka Ashram where I got such a startling message from the Almighty God. When I first met Lucile, I felt almost as if she were a Korean, although she is an American through-and-through, with her looks and mannerisms, so I was especially delighted to accept her invitation.

I arrived in Annapolis and we greeted each other as if we had been friends all our lives. This is the great tie found in the love of God.

The Sewells have two daughters and one son, Dr. William H. Sewell, a noted cardiac surgeon at Guthrie Clinic, Sayre, Pennsylvania. He designed and made a heart pump in his student days which is now displayed at the Smithsonian. He is a genius in this field, and has

115

written many books and articles. Above all, he has saved many lives with his skill and devotion.

Lucile Sewell is a graduate of Randolph-Macon Women's College in Lynchburg, Virginia, where William F. Quillian, Jr., is now president. His father was president of Wesleyan College when I was a student there. Four generations in Lucile's family—her father, her daughter, her grandaughter, and herself—are all members of Phi Beta Kappa.

I spent two nights with the Sewells. When I went into the dining room for breakfast, I found a gift check for our school on the table—a $5000 check! I almost screamed with joy for two reasons. First, it was my birthday, although they had not known it. Second, that was almost exactly the amount we needed to finish the first two stories of the vocational high school building. I repeated again, "Is there anything too hard for me?" God proved what he said through the Russells and the Sewells, with their generous contributions.

Since my Upper Room experience at Lasell House, somehow, some way, God has always given me the material needs in connection with my school—not one penny more or less—just the right amount in each case.

Such noticeable wonders take place constantly since I decided not to charge for my speeches following my spiritual rebirth. You will recall why I left the whole matter in the hands of God. Whatever is given for my work by speaking or the sale of my books has always been blessed by God.

I cannot help but think of George Mueller, a great English preacher in the nineteenth century. One day, with much prayer, George Mueller determined not to take any salary, never to ask any human being for help, and to take literally the biblical commands "Sell what you possess and give it to the poor," and "Owe no man anything."

He wished to start an orphans' home, but he con-

116

fided his desire to God alone. He wrote in his journal. "Today I have had it very much laid on my heart. No longer merely to *think* about the establishment of an orphans' home, but actually to *set* about it, and I have been much in prayer respecting it in order to ascertain the Lord's mind. *I have been much in prayer* yesterday and today about the orphans' home, and am more and more convinced that it is of God. May He in mercy guide me. The chief three reasons are: (1) That God may be glorified, should He be pleased to furnish me with the means in its being seen that it is not a vain thing to trust him: and that thus the faith of His children may be strengthened; (2) the spiritual welfare of fatherless and motherless children; (3) their temporal welfare."

After some months of prayer and waiting on God, he was able to rent a house with room for thirty children, and in the course of time rented three more, caring for one hundred twenty children. The work was carried on in this way for ten years. The supplies for the needs of these orphans were asked and received of God alone. It was often a time of sore need and much prayer, but he never ceased to praise, honor, and glorify God.

He was led to desire and to wait upon God, and eventually he received from him the sure promise of all things needful to care for more than two thousand homeless children.

It is a constant wonder the way God opens doors for me as he did for George Mueller. Faith and work—work and faith—the two cannot be separated.

It has been fifteen years since I was first invited to the Keuka Ashram at Keuka College in New York, by Mrs. William M. Passano, whose husband was then director. Since that time, Ida Passano and I have gone to Lasell House together several times during the Ascensiontide and Whitsuntide Retreats in May.

William and Ida Passano went to Korea in the fall

117

of 1964, soon after our school was founded. Neither Iris nor I was there to greet them, but they saw the school in its beginning stage. Upon their return to America, Ida Passano gave a tea for more than one hundred of her friends. She asked me to speak about our school—the purpose behind it, how it was established, and how it was being supported.

It was the Christmas season and people wanted to share. Checks started coming—from three to sixty dollars each. The total reached more than five hundred dollars. Some continued to contribute for several years afterward.

I receive generous support from many church-school classes. Two are especially active in my behalf. One is the Ladies' Bible Class of St. David's United Church in Toronto, Canada, which Ethel Dean and Doris Cortice attend. These two friends went with me on my first Orient tour and are Canadian representatives on our foundation board. I met them originally at a "Camp Farthest Out" in Ontario in 1957, and have visited them every year since then. Ethel's four sisters are as devoted to the Ladies' Bible Class as she is.

The class membership is not more than thirty-five, but they do wonders with money-making projects. Each year they have a "talent drive," where they sell the work of their hands. They have annual fund-raising dinners and give generously from their own pockets, as well. The class raises approximately $9000 a year, which they divide among the Canadian Bible Society, in memory of their first teacher, and many other worthy projects. Our foundation receives at least $500 a year. In 1974, we were given more than $2000.

The other women's Bible class which gives us continuing support is Burrall Class in Calvary Baptist Church, Washington, D.C., taught by Margaret K. Patterson for fifteen years. The class is large enough to be a small church, with more than one hundred members.

They have a Christmas project each year to raise money for those in need. Twice we have been given $1000, once before we started building the school and once afterward. In addition, the class gives a scholarship each year.

For many years, Miss Patterson was principal of the Lafayette Elementary School, a few blocks from our home, which my two grandsons attended. One year she won a $10,000 house in Forida by entering a "twenty-five words or less" contest on the topic "What do you want most out of life after thirty-five?" I do not know anyone else who made $400 a word as Margaret Patterson did; therefore, I seek her advice when I prepare my Christmas letters. Both Iris and I feel blessed that Iris's sons received their important elementary education under her supervision. Often, I can see her influence in their words, thoughts, and actions.

Of all the gifts and contributions I have received over a long period of time for Berea in Korea, two are unique. The first was a check for $200 from a friend, Helen Blague of Springfield, Massachusetts. She is a music teacher and a member of the United Church of Christ Faith Church. Her Faith Church Guild has been loyal to our foundation with contribution checks twice a year for many years. Mrs. Blague told me that this particular contribution came from her father, the late Dr. Homer D. Hulbert, who went to Korea at the request of Korea's last king to open a school for the sons and daughters of nobles.

When Japan annexed Korea, Dr. Hulbert returned to America and wrote a book *The History of Korea*. His dearest wish—to return to Korea—was realized in 1949, after Korea's independence, but he died eight days after arriving in Seoul. The American consul sent his belongings to his daughter who discovered that he had not used $200 worth of traveler's checks. In the confusion, the checks were mislaid. Twenty years later Mrs. Blague found them and was happy to discover they could still be redeemed. Her brothers agreed enthusiastically to give the money to our school. So God sent us a gift from a dead man; the spirit of Dr. Hulbert's love for Korea goes on, through our school.

The other gift came from Dulin United Methodist Church in Falls Church, Virginia, which our foundation secretary, Lily Houseman, attends. Instead of the usual poinsettia memorials on Christmas Sunday, members of her church contributed to our school in memory or in honor of dear ones. Thus, Dulin departed from a traditional observance in favor of practical action and sent a check for $220. It was deposited in the Berea in Korea Endowment Fund established in 1972 by Lily and her husband Earl Houseman. The fund is growing through the efforts of their family, friends, and various organizations to which they belong. One organization we share, and whose members are most generous in support of our work, is the Kappa Phi Club for University Christian Women.

How different our Christian faith is from Buddhism. Buddhism teaches noninvolvement and withdrawal from life. In the special gifts mentioned above, not only the living but also those long dead are involved in our school work.

Among different kinds of gifts that we receive, that of scholarships plays a very important part in the lives of our students. A year's tuition for the Vocational High School is $120. Some individuals and organizations regularly give this amount. It is a favorite means of contributing for Sunday School classes who might send ten dollars a month; others send quarterly or semiannual installments. Our faculty members give two scholarships each year from their own meager salaries. We are pleased to be able to offer more scholarships to needy and worthy students than any other school in Seoul.

As I write about the special or unique gifts, I also

offer heartfelt thanks to the hundreds of friends, individually and collectively through churches, service organizations and foundations, who are involved in our work—men, women, children; Americans, Canadians, Koreans. Some have sent memorial gifts or bequeathed sums in their wills. Others have purchased annuities. I owe a great debt to all my friends in the United States of America and Canada who have assisted me all these years so faithfully and loyally, without fail, like the morning sunrise each day.

My fund-raising reached a climax with a grant from the U.S. Agency for International Development (A.I.D.) in June, 1973. Truthfully, I thought A.I.D. transactions took place between two governments, and never gave it a thought. Therefore, I was surprised when a friend suggested that I go to the State Department to discuss a grant with Arturo Costantino in the Office of American Schools and Hospitals Abroad. Although I had never met him or heard of his work, I made an appointment for 3:00 that afternoon.

On the same day, Iris and I were invited to lunch at the Kennedy Center by Frances and Esther Van Dyne of the Chevy Chase United Methodist Church. These two sisters live according to the teachings of the Bible: generous, unassuming, and sharing. We affectionately call them St. Frances and Queen Esther, whose qualities they share.

After lunch, they dropped us off at the State Department. We were met by four men in the Office of American Schools and Hospitals Abroad: Arturo Costantino, Michael Codi, Eugene Tucci, and David Santos. I felt at home right away because the office was small and comfortable and the men were friendly. I can always sense the temperature of a group, hot or cold, when I walk in. The temperature of this office was just right for me!

Iris and I were prepared with brochures and con-

struction plans for the building, so urgently needed for our vocational high school. Mr. Constantino gave us the application forms for an A.I.D. grant—ten sheets of legal size. We were to fill them out in triplicate.

No deadline was set; so, when we returned home, I simply put them on the desk and looked at the pile. It was so formidable! Iris left for Korea shortly thereafter, and I went to Florida to fulfill a number of speaking engagements. I mentioned the application for an A.I.D. grant to several friends, but the reaction was disheartening. They told me it would be as difficult as finding a needle in a haystack. I would need a strong magnet to find it.

I knew we had a strong magnet—so strong that it could hoist even the earth. Our magnet is God.

When I arrived home on March 5, my first telephone call was from Michael Codi. He told me time was running out for the A.I.D. application.

Immediately, I called Lily Houseman, our foundation secretary. "Lily, I need you, but most of all, I *need* your husband. Can you come right away?"

An hour later they were at my door, and in five hours we finished the application form. The next day I submitted it in person to the Office of American Schools and Hospitals Abroad. Then, with a special prayer for A.I.D., I left on another speaking trip.

My last trip for the season was in Arkansas, where I was leader for the young people of the Arkansas "Camp Farthest Out," in Fayetteville. Little Rock is my second home in that area, because Mrs. Thelma W. Kenney and her sister Mrs. James R. Jones live there. I first met Thelma Kenney many years ago on Long Island, New York. After the death of her husband, she went back to her home state where she worked for the Welcome Wagon, supervising Arkansas and the neighboring states. She introduced me to her friends through her church and the American Business Women's Association of Arkansas and Louisiana.

Once again, the first call upon my return to Washington came from the Office of American Schools and Hospitals Abroad. It was Michael Codi who said, "Mrs. Pahk, could you come to the office on June 13 at 4:30 P.M.?"

I replied, "I will."

It was a very hot day. At exactly 4:30, I was escorted into Mr. Constantino's office, and sat alone on the sofa facing all four men. I was still unaware of what was coming.

Mr. Constantino said, "Mrs. Pahk, we are prepared to give the Berea in Korea Foundation a grant of $300,000. Will you sign it?"

As I was ecstatically signing my name, I offered a thanksgiving prayer for America—thus far, my individual American friends supported me, but now the American people collectively support Berea in Korea, because grant money comes from the people's taxes.

With this grant, we were able to add two additional stories to "Morning Glory," the vocational high school building and to install a heating plant, all within six months.

However, before construction could begin, the State Department required blueprints and specifications. My first duty after securing the grant was to find a consulting architect. I called on my next-door neighbor William G. Hughes and presented the problem. He told me another neighbor, Donald J. Neubauer, was in that field. We had a "garden acquaintance" with his family.

Don Neubauer was more than glad to give advice on our blueprints. He was a structural engineer for the great flight cage at the National Zoological Park in Washington, D.C., an imaginative structure built of steel for beauty and economy. Soaring to ninety feet, it provides plenty of airspace for birds to stretch their wings, while rocks, waterfalls, trees, and shrubbery make them feel at home.

This structure was cited for "excellent engineering"

by the American Iron and Steel Institute in 1964. How blessed our foundation is to have Mr. Neubauer as consulting architect!

On January 20, 1974 (Korean New Year's Day), Iris welcomed Mr. Costantino and Donald Richbourg from the State Department, and Marion Edwards, brother of the governor of Louisiana, to our campus in Seoul. It was snow-covered, white, and sparkling in the sun, but very cold. It was a proud moment for our school.

In the presence of Arturo Costantino, I had signed the grant six months previously, and now he saw the finished product, with a plaque reading: "The additional two floors of this building, including central heating for the entire building of the Induk Vocational High School in Seoul, Korea, was made possible by the generous grant from the U.S. Agency for International Development (A.I.D.), November, 1973."

In addition to the construction, we were able to buy $100,000 worth of machinery and equipment for the classroom workshops. Forty thousand dollars was used for strengthening the staff. It permitted us to employ William F. Dresselhaus, a graduate in engineering and design from Iowa State and Stanford Universities, as an associate professor for a fifteen-month period, and to bring Chul-Soo Kim and Hong Park to America to study and observe for three months at Pratt Institute, New York; Illinois Institute of Technology; and Art Center College, Los Angeles, California. The presence of Bill Dresselhaus and these two teachers has charged the atmosphere on our campus with challenge and hope. This is one of the most effective ways of building a friendship bridge between Korea and America.

We used the grant well, multiplying its effect. But we needed a college workshop urgently. Our college students were forced to use the high school workshop, which caused much overcrowding. We had made an application for a second grant from A.I.D. I had been in-

124

formed that there was little hope for one in 1975, but I trusted God absolutely and left the whole matter to him.

One morning in the spring of 1974, I had awakened with a dream. I seldom dream, but when I do it is significant and prophetic. In this dream, I was boarding an ocean liner. Everyone else went in ahead of me—I was the last one in line. I knew I had to present my ticket, but I couldn't find it. I fished through my pocketbook with no success. At that moment, two men who stood beside me told the ticket officer, "Let her on."

Without further question, he let me pass. The room was already full except for two empty seats. As I started to take one, a young man came up and said, "You have a room by yourself."

He escorted me to a large lounge facing the sea and left me alone. I sat in a comfortable chair looking at the blue water and thanked God, "You let me in without a ticket."

In a few minutes the young man returned with my dinner. It was a sizzling T-bone steak! I knew then that we would get another grant.

A little more than a year later, I received a telephone call, but I did not understand what was said so I answered, "Wrong number."

The voice at the other end said, "Isn't this Induk Pahk's number?"

I agreed that it was and was told that because we had made such good use of our first grant, A.I.D. had allotted the Berea in Korea Foundation $250,000 for the new fiscal year.

I hung up the phone repeating, "Wrong number! Thank you, God."

Meanwhile, we had decided to sell some of our school property which had been cut off from the main campus by a public road. The value of the land was very low. Then suddenly a miracle took place. With the coming of the Seoul subway to within a mile of our campus, land prices rose sharply. Iris did not lose the chance. She immediately sold our excess land.

The opportunity to sell lasted but a short time. The government set aside that entire area as a green belt and no one could buy or sell.

But our sale had already been made! Both Iris and I had always wanted a chapel combined with an auditorium. At present, the largest room we have is the dining room, seating three hundred. With increasing enrollment, we need a building large enough to seat at least eight hundred. Now, with money from the sale of the land, our dream could become a reality. No longer would our graduation ceremonies and our entrance exercises for seven hundred twenty new students have to be out-of-doors, at the mercy of the unpredictable March weather. We could all praise God together!

Even if I had a thousand tongues, I could not praise God enough!

CHAPTER X

That which you are seeking—if from God—is seeking you!

—Induk Pahk

I am from the old country of Korea with its long history of more than four thousand years. The first six years and two months I was brought up in the age-old, traditional way by a Buddhist mother and a Confucian father. As a child I couldn't even laugh aloud; I was stopped by my mother, saying, "A girl should not laugh like a boy." I was not allowed to play with boys because it was taboo. The weight of the old tradition was too heavy for any Korean to lift.

But a miracle took place! The Christian faith took hold of my Buddhist mother after my father's death. The light of God brightened her path, and she boldly left the 4000-year-old traditional way. Mother and I were freed from the cage and flew above in the sky like eagles.

An ancient legend concerning the eagle tells us that it has a remarkable peculiarity among birds: when a severe storm occurs, all other birds do one of two things—either they hide from the storm in the lee of a convenient natural shelter, or they try to fight it as long as their strength holds out. The eagle neither fights a storm nor runs away, but soars above it. My mother was like the eagle. She soared above all the knotty and weighty problems when she saw the light of Jesus Christ on Christmas Day. She always used to say, "It was a miracle." I agreed with her. It was the first, but not the last, miracle in my life.

The thing that is important in a miracle is not that something extraordinary has happened which we cannot explain; the important thing is that *God acts*. God has been performing miracles in my life—one after another, ever since.

With my coming to America as a student in 1926, the new page in the history of my life turned lightly without my knowledge of what was in store. Of course, I had a dream but it was a million miles away then.

In my days at Ewha, I learned something about American history, but I did not know the life of the American people until I came and mingled with the students, their families, and their churches.

Gradually, I learned who came to America and settled it. I learned that Christianity has been deeply influenced by the Anglo-Saxon heritage. The Norsemen, ancestors of the Anglo-Saxon people, dwelt on the rugged coast of Norway. They got most of their living from the sea; but it was not sufficient, so they also had to cultivate those rugged hillsides. It was a precarious existence and could sustain only a limited number. When the sons came on, they were compelled to launch out for themselves. The hillsides could not sustain them, and they could not push the hills back to make more room; their only outlet was to sail away to distant lands.

Some eventually landed on the new continent of America, perhaps after a long interval in Britain. Out of this social inheritance came three great characteristics: self-reliance; aggressiveness, and the love of individual freedom. Each family became self-sufficient and depended little upon the settled community.

The word *aggressiveness* implies action. When I

think of Christianity, action comes to my mind. Coming from a country where both Confucianism and Buddhism have been passive and inactive, the word itself awakened me from a dormant stage—suddenly a refreshing gale blew through my whole being. By a flash of illumination, I caught a vision—a school for Korean youth. God has a plan for everyone, and he has one for me, too; this is it—to build a school.

One's life is a dash between two dates, the date of birth and the date of death. When I first visited an old Episcopal graveyard in Alabama, I noticed all the tombstones were inscribed with a name; and underneath was the date of birth, a dash, then the date of death. One particular tombstone read: "She did the best she could." What a significant statement that was! Those six words described the quality of her life. That was her "dash" line.

The dash line may be divided into four parts like the four seasons in a man's life:

1–25:   *Springtime*—the age of preparation, of sowing seeds. He learns from his parents at home, from teachers in school and church. He has dreams and visions, hopes and ideals.
25–45: *Summertime*—the age of working and cultivating. His dreams and plans are gradually unfolding. He is involved in family, church, and community.
45–65: *Autumn*—the age of reaping and storing up the harvest. His dreams are realized.
65–   : *Wintertime*—the age for enjoying the harvest.

This book recounts the first two stages of my life, and some phases of the third stage; although from the standpoint of age, I am in the fourth stage.

If I am to fulfill my destiny, the cock still has to crow! But I could not crow had I not perfect health! We have a saying, "Even if you give me gold, I cannot do the task because physically I am not equal to it."

I am still equal to my task! God gave me four marvelous gifts to help me realize my flash of illumination: my daughter Iris, my friends, my health, and his blessings. I feel I have everything needed for this important work for which God commissioned me.

I am reminded of the story of a seventy-five-year-old man who went to the doctor for a check-up. He was given a clean slate and asked, "What makes you so healthy at your age?"

The old man answered, "My wife and I have been married for fifty years. From the beginning we decided that when we quarreled, my wife would go to the kitchen and I would take a walk. Since then, I've taken a lot of walks."

I don't have to walk to keep my health, but I do a lot of traveling, meeting people, making new friends, speaking and listening, learning and getting new ideas such as "give value to that which has no value by your own ingenuity," or "make the ordinary extraordinary." Besides, my friends teach me new words, expressions, idioms, and even jokes. When a proper occasion arises, I repeat jokes I have heard with all my enthusiasm. When the expected laughter does not come, I know I have lost the punch line!

Over a period of time, through many difficulties, my mind has become resilient yet resolute, and I have learned to bend—otherwise, I would break. Someone once said, "The mark of leadership is the ability to make adjustments." When I face a difficult situation or a serious problem, I take it as my own refinery to purify my character—shaking off and burning up the negative side of my life. My mother taught me to use my mistakes as fertilizer for a more abundant crop in the future.

I want to be faithful to God and my friends, like the characters in the following legend.

In the olden times in Korea, the wives of two very

130

close friends were expecting babies. They wanted their children to marry each other when they grew up if they were different sexes, and it so happened that they were. Of course, both children were told that they were betrothed, but they were not allowed to see each other as they were growing up.

As time went on, the boy's family became poor and moved away. A rich family in the village asked for the girl's hand. The girl's father told his wife his decision: "The first boy's family become poor and went away to an unknown place. Here is a rich family that wants our daughter as a bride for their son. We should not miss such an opportune chance. Get ready for a wedding!"

He did not consult with his wife about this matter, but just commanded it, dogmatically. That was the way our family life ran for centuries.

While the two families were busy preparing for the wedding, the girl quietly disappeared. Of course, the parents were shocked and the gossip among the villagers was unbearable. Some said the bride-to-be had a lover and ran away with him.

Where did the bride-to-be go? She wanted to be faithful to the man to whom she was engaged while still in her mother's womb. So she fled alone to a Buddhist nunnery, shaved her head, and became a full-fledged nun.

Meanwhile, the young man returned to the village after his parents' deaths to claim his promised bride. He was told that she had been married into a rich family. In great disappointment and despondency, he renounced the world and entered a Buddhist temple, shaved his head, and became a monk.

Neither the girl nor the young man knew the other was living secluded in a Buddhist temple, completely withdrawn from the world, hoping to meet the other in the next world when they were reincarnated.

One Summer day, just as the sun was going down,

the nun, with a sack on her back and a cane in her hand, was returning from a village where she had gone to seek alms. She sat down to rest where the road forked—one branch leading to the nunnery, the other to the monastery.

As she meditated, there came a monk with a sack on his back and a cane in his hand. By this time, both were old. They greeted each other.

The monk said, "Why did you become a nun?"

She unfolded her story. Then she asked in turn, "Why did you become a monk?"

As he told his story they realized that they were the very persons who were betrothed when they were in their mother's wombs, sixty-five years before. For fifty years, from the time she had reached marriageable age, she had thought only of him, and vice versa. No one else came into their minds but each other for half a century.

As the sun was setting, it was time for them to return to their respective temples. Together, they vowed to reincarnate as husband and wife and live together in the next life. He let her depart first, watching her until the shadows of dusk enveloped her.

Some years later, travelers along the road to the Diamond Mountains where both temples were located noticed an unusually beautiful pair of butterflies—two velvety-gray butterflies, hovering around each other at the fork in the road.

They are seen there each August, nowhere else. People say they are the reincarnated nun and monk, faithful for eternity.

This story is a legend, but the moral is noteworthy! I want to be faithful in what I am doing, no matter how meager and insignificant it seems. Success comes when consistency of purpose is united with faithfulness to the work.

Two frogs fell into a pail of cream. One gave up,

sank to the bottom, and drowned. The other paddled with such force that by-and-by there was a lump of butter giving him something to stand on and making it possible for him to leap over the top.

This is the end of my thirty-third year of speaking, and I have been doing a lot of paddling like the latter frog, with one goal—to make a lump of butter so I could leap over the top. Why? To help Korea to be strong through educating her young people.

I have been in every state of the Union and every province in Canada, crossing North America, from the Atlantic to the Pacific, seventy-two times; I have come to the United States of America twenty-one times. I have traveled enough mileage to make three round trips to the moon; by the time this book is published, I could be on the moon for the fourth time. A friend of mine said, "Oh, you will crow from the moon!"

So far, I have spoken 6808 times in all states except five: Alaska, Nevada, North Dakota, Utah, and Wyoming, and in all the provinces in Canada except Newfoundland. Since I have a standing invitation from Anchorage, I can stop there on my way to Korea to speak anytime. But I have wondered why I did not get invitations from the other four states . . .

I have come to my own conclusions concerning the reasons: North Dakota is Lawrence Welk's state, so I don't have to go. Wyoming is Buffalo Bill's, and I would not have any room to roam. Utah is a Mormon state, and they don't need me. Nevada is a gambling state, and they don't want me—they don't know what an expert international gambler I am!

When I started construction on our first two buildings, I needed more cash than I had on hand, so with great daring—for one as inexperienced in finance as I was—I entered the international wool market, buying raw wool from a company in Australia and selling it to a woolen mill in Seoul. I made a good profit on the

133

deal—exactly what I needed to complete the school buildings!

I am willing to follow wherever God leads in pursuit of the goal he has set for me. The material needs for Berea in Korea have been met in many ways and through many agencies, both in North America and in Korea.

The tapestry of my life will not be complete without a four-year college of design; that picture in the tapestry is just half-woven. A two-year college, Induk Institute of Design, was started in 1972 with one hundred young men and women exploring in three areas: industrial, commercial, and environmental design. The college is the brainchild of my daughter Iris; it is the first school of its kind in Korean history. There are separate art schools and technical schools, but no other institution combines these schools as ours does.

Induk Schools are located on the northeastern edge of Seoul; the Seoul College of Technology is just across the valley—a road and railroad run between them.

Korea has her own color, shape, and form, in the field of art as exemplified in the unexcelled porcelain produced in the reign of the Korea Dynasty. She also has excellent-quality clay for making chinaware, as well as fine-quality silk. We can design and make new articles by using more of our old skills and by studying the new ideas from other countries, thus creating something beautiful, useful, and reasonable.

Our concept for teaching creative design combines school, workshop, studio, and laboratory. This new school stimulates and challenges those who have practical ability and creative imagination which has lain dormant much too long.

Our college motto, like that of our high school, is "With Hand and Head, Create Something Out of Nothing." We hope that this new venture will be a great and unique service to Korea for generations to come and to mankind as a whole.

134

In three years of experience, we have found that two years of junior college is only enough to break the ice. Our students need at least four years to become qualified designers. Thus, our goal has been expanded to encompass a four-year college. I have no doubt God will see me through, because he never lets me down.

When Iris was dreaming and planning for a junior college, I had a vision one midmorning in April, 1970, at my home. Iris came home that Chistmas and said that she would apply for permission to start the college. She followed up on her plans prayerfully after she returned to Seoul. At about the same time, I saw a vision. I went into my kitchen for a glass of water and saw through the window two mushroom-shaped columns of smoke, of grayish white smoke, one taller than the other, through the screen on the back porch. I was alarmed, thinking something was burning, although I could not imagine what it could be.

Strangest of all, the two columns of smoke were absolutely still—not moving at all. I opened the door to the back porch to investigate what it was all about, but the two columns were gone. They had simply vanished. It all took place in less than thirty seconds. I knew then that we would get permission for a junior college of design, because the tall smoke column represented a junior college, and the smaller one our vocational high school.

The following August, I arrived at Haneda International Airport in Tokyo. Iris came from Taiwan, and we met at the Pan American ticket counter. The first thing she said was, "Mother, our application for a junior college fell through."

"It did?" I responded. Then I continued, "But you will be asked to make an application again."

She replied, "How can you be so affirmative?"

I answered, "When God steps in, no one can stop it. Just wait for his action—a miracle."

I was right. In November of that same year, Iris was asked to make another application for a junior college of

135

design by the Ministry of Education which had vetoed it three months previously. She brought the permit with her when she came to our Annual Board Meeting in January, 1971. Now we had our foot in the door, and I am sure we will get a permit for a four-year college of design when we apply for it.

The Berea in Korea Foundation has excellent Boards of Directors, one in Washington, D.C., the other in Seoul, where it is called Induk School Foundation. The American Board of Directors takes care of financial matters, the Korean handles policies.

Our American Board consists of five members: Charles R. Hughes, M.D., treasurer—brilliant, calm, and collected, always on an even keel: Lily Houseman, secretary—a person of ingenuity and action: Iris Kim, vice-president; Joseph Lee (Iris's older son), second vice-president; and myself, president.

We hold our annual meeting on the first Wednesday in January. Iris returns from Seoul for this meeting each year. Margery Hughes, wife of the Treasurer, and Earl Houseman, husband of the secretary, attend as ex-officio members, and Margaret K. Patterson serves as representative for our eighteen advisors.

We always start our board meeting by singing, "How Great Thou Art." Margery Hughes, an accomplished musician, plays and leads the singing. From the beginning, we feel the presence of God who is the head of our foundation.

I am also president of the Korean Board. The acting-president, in my absence, is Dr. Chai-Yu Choi, who was minister of education under Syngman Rhee's administration. Not only is his experience valuable to us, but he is just like my own brother and treats our school as his own. Both Boards are faithful and furnish their best ideas. "My cup runneth over!"

The eighteen American advisors and three Canadian representatives of our foundation also contribute in many ways. One of them is Dr. Kenneth H. Thompson of Berea College, Berea, Kentucky. When I wanted to bring one of our teachers to Berea College, I presented the proposition to Dr. Thompson, dean of instruction and foreign student advisor. He worked out a plan for Jung-Il Kim to come to Berea on a working aid scholarship. It was one of the thrilling moments of my life when I stepped off the Greyhound bus at Berea College on June 27, 1975, and was met by Dr. and Mrs. Thompson and Jung-Il Kim.

It took me thirty-five years to start Berea in Korea; and now, twelve years later, one of our own teachers has actually come to Berea College to study.

Dr. Thompson has served at Berea for nineteen years. Prior to joining the staff, he served as director of teacher training in Moga, Punjab, India, at the School for Village Teachers. During his sabbatical year, 1955, Dean Thompson was executive secretary and leader of the secondary education team for the U. S. Educational Foundation in Pakistan. With all of his great success, he has a genuine interest in our school and would not only go to the second mile for us, but also the third and fourth if we needed him.

In the midst of working out our goals in life, both Iris and I went through some tempestuous moments with Joong Hee (now Joseph) and Sun Hee. It was Mrs. Julia Clews who helped us, through prayer, to weather the stormy years. She is married to Dr. Hedley Clews, a noted Methodist minister.

For a long time, Julia and I have been "prayer partners." Our mutual prayer project for a number of years was my two grandsons and her son Bill, when they were all teenagers.

I recall the day Julia telephoned me and broke the news, "Induk, praise God! Bill is going to marry a lovely girl." In this day and age, that one sentence means a lot.

Both Joseph and Sun Hee have since found their own places in life, yet they have not forgotten their mother and grandmother.

During their early years, I once asked my elder grandson, "Joong, what comes to your mind when you think of grandma?"

Without hesitation he pointed out my theme song, as he replied, "My God, My God, My School, My School!"

Then some weeks later, I asked the same question of my second grandson; I was curious as to what he would say. I asked, "Sun, what comes to your mind when you think of grandma?"

He, too, without hesitation, slowly and emphatically said, "Work . . . work . . . work!"

My two grandsons caught the essence of my life! I could not have said it any better.

According to the Oriental animal signs, when a person is born under the sign of the rooster, as I am, he is destined to do some pioneering and exploring. Like a rooster announcing the new day, the person knows what is coming. He makes a careful study of the situation as a surgeon explores a wound. Yet, undertaking pioneer work involves danger and unknown risks. To me that unknown factor is exciting and challenging. A pioneer's mission is to be the first to open an unknown territory for others to travel. What a thrilling opportunity!

I love to get up early when I am at home to hear the birds sing and to praise my Creator with them. Mother was an early riser; she used to say, "Who wants to breathe air that has already been used? I want fresh air that no one has breathed ahead of me."

The rooster heralds each dawn—the beginning of a new day, a new hope. Dawn is exciting to watch! Slowly, it creeps over mountain and prairie, over ocean and island; it lifts the dark curtain of night and brings light to the world. I have seen it countless times. What magic it is! One can see all the millions of objects newly created with the dawn. It is the time when the birds start singing.

The cock is king of the barnyard! His crowing in

the early morning has served as an alarm clock to farmers for thousands of years. It still does in the many places of our world where clocks and watches are a rarity.

Of all the cocks that have crowed since time immemorial, there is one cock who crowed on time, not one minute ahead or one minute late—exactly on the dot, to accentuate a great event in human history. It was the cock that crowed the night Jesus was arrested by his enemies, to be crucified:

> Jesus said to him [the disciple Peter], "Truly, I say to you, this very night, before the cock crows, you will deny me three times."
>
> Peter said to Him, "Even if I must die with you, I will not deny you." And so said all the disciples. . . .
>
> . . . Then all the disciples forsook Him and fled. . . .
>
> Now Peter was sitting outside in the courtyard. And a maid came up to him, and said, "You also were with Jesus the Galilean."
>
> But he denied it before them all, saying, "I do not know what you mean."
>
> And when he went out to the porch, another maid saw him, and she said to the bystanders." This man was with Jesus of Nazareth."
>
> And again he denied it with an oath, "I do not know the man."
>
> After a little while the bystanders came up and said to Peter, "Certainly you are also one of them, for your accent betrays you."
>
> Then he began to invoke a curse on himself and to swear, "I do not know the man." And immediately the cock crowed.
>
> And Peter remembered the saying of Jesus, "Before the cock crows, you will deny me three times." And he went out and wept bitterly.

—Matthew 26:34–35, 56, 69–75, RSV

Indeed, the cock crowed on time and changed cowardly Peter into a strong man like a rock; and on that rock foundation, Jesus promised to build His church.

The year 1976 is my fiftieth year since I first came to America. It is my Jubilee Year! In the Old Testament (Leviticus 25:8), every fiftieth year was a time to proclaim liberty throughout the land to all enslaved debtors and a time for the cancelling of all public and private debts—free from all the debts. What a happy year that must have been!

Likewise, I feel free and happy in my fiftieth year in America. It was only through the American Christian missionaries that I learned the secret of being liberated and fulfilled. I want to share it, on a universal basis, with all you readers so that you, too, may enjoy your Jubilee!

On my journey through life, what has prompted my crowing? My God, my school, my work, my family and friends!

I have had a very adventurous past. It is now history, but I am looking ahead to a more glorious future and adventure which is still a mystery.

For that mystery, I will keep on crowing—looking to Jesus, the pioneer and perfector of our faith!

INDEX

Lee, Joong Hee (Joseph), 40–41, 49, 136, 137, 138
Lee, Rubie, 19
Lee, Sun Hee, 40–41, 49, 137, 138
Lewis, C. Pendleton, 6–7

Maeser, Dr. Karl G., 53
Maine, 50, 51, 113
Massachusetts, 53, 54, 76, 84, 119
Marquis, Mrs. T. L., 90
Martin, Elva E., 94
Martin, Mary Lou, 78
Maryland, 115
Methodist Missionaries, 3, 8–10, 12, 14, 24, 91, 140
Michelangelo, 4, 81
Michigan, 22, 26, 94
Mitchell, Howard and Grace, 50–51
Monyangtul, 45
Mormons, 52–53
Mother, 2, 7–8, 13–14, 17, 19, 21, 24, 28, 35, 36, 45–46, 127, 130, 138
Moving a Mountain, 93–94
Mueller, George, 116–17
Music, Korean, 62–63

Neill, Eleanor, 22
Neubauer, Donald, 123–24
Nevada, 133
New Hampshire, 48–51, 53–54
New Jersey, 75
New Village Movement, 110
New York, 117, 124
New York Times, 76
North Dakota, 133

Ohio, 43, 77, 94
Ohio Wesleyan University, 7, 11, 14
Oliver Twist, 82
Ondol Room, 103–4
Oriental Symbols of Longevity, 59
Oriental Zodiac, 2, 36, 138

Pae Chae Boys' High School, 11, 12
Pangborn, Martha, 43–44
Panmunjom, 106
Park Chung Hee, 90
Park Chung Hee, Madame, 97

Park, Hong, 124
Passano, Ida, 117–18
Passano, William, 117
Patterson, Margaret K., 94, 118–19, 136
Pennsylvania, 9, 29, 56, 67, 79, 91, 115
Permanent Visa, 78
Pope, Mildred, 94
Port Chinnampo, 45
Pratt Institute, 124
Protestant Radio and Television Center, 114
Pusan, Korea, 41, 114

Quillian, Dr. Wm. F., 25–26
Quillian, Mrs. W. F., 21–22
Quillian, W. F. Jr., 116

Randolph-Macon Women's College, 116
Resurrection Gate, 92
Richbourg, Donald, 124
Rhode Island, 38, 72
Robinson, Ruth, 55
Root, Mary Catherine, 54–55
Royal Examinations, 28, 100
Russell, Ellen, 87
Russell, Harlow, 114–16
Russell, Ruth, 113, 114–15
Russia, 60

Santos, David, 121
Scranton, Mary, 3, 60–61, 91
Seoul, Korea, 3, 9, 10, 28, 32, 44, 54, 57, 63, 75, 90–91, 96–97, 107, 109, 111, 119, 124, 126, 133–34
September Monkey, 9, 50, 75–79
Sewell, Dr. William F., Jr., 115
Sewell, Lucile, 115–16
Sewell, William F., 115–16
Shin, Dr. Pong Cho, 96
Skidmore, Marie and Merwyn, 94
South Carolina, 54
Spiritual Rebirth, 86–90, 116
Stanford University, 124
Steinhart, C. G., 9, 77
Stevens, The Rev. Florence, 38, 41

143